40 Successful Personal Statements

with an introduction and comments by
Guy Nobes and Gavin Nobes, Ph.D.

D0294105

COA
opening doors of opportunity

40 Successful Personal Statements

This edition published in 2006 by Cambridge Occupational Analysts Ltd
Sparham, Norwich, NR9 5PR

Editorial and Publishing Team

Introduction and Comments Guy Nobes and Gavin Nobes, Ph.D.
Copy Editor Ken Reynolds
Commissioning Publishing Editor John Mainstone
Design and typesetting Simon Foster

British Library Cataloguing in Publication Data
A catalogue record for this book is available from the British Library.

ISBN 0-9550541-2-5

Typeset by Cambridge Occupational Analysts Ltd, Sparham, Norwich NR9 5PR
Printed and bound in Great Britain by Clays Ltd, Bungay, Suffolk NR35 1ED

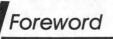# Foreword

Acknowledgements

Many thanks to the pupils who generously agreed to have their personal statements published so that future generations may have a less fraught experience.

Our debt is great also to the following admissions experts:

Dr Steve P Townsend, University of Aberdeen;

Beth Gorman and Claire Powell, Bristol University;

Dr Geoff Parks and Emer Scott, University of Cambridge;

Ruth Miller, University of Durham;

Kelly Campbell, Glasgow University;

Catherine Smethurst, University of Leicester;

Rachel Cook, University of Manchester;

Brigitte Burrows, Queen Mary, University of London;

Helen Charlesworth, Oxford University

and Brian Heap, author of 'Degree Course Offers'.

Biographies

Guy Nobes is Head of Higher Education & Careers at Marlborough College.

Dr Gavin Nobes is a Principal Lecturer at the University of East London

Contents

40 SUCCESSFUL PERSONAL STATEMENTS
15

The page references are given in order of the statement's coverage of the course.

THIS BOOK IS:

- **a collection of forty successful personal statements** from applications that have won offers or places from a wide range of institutions in a variety of the most popular subjects

- **designed to inspire and guide** you as you square up to writing what for most people is the most difficult and daunting part to the application - the personal statement

- **meant to demystify** the personal statement, by explaining and illustrating what admissions tutors actually want

- **intended to help you assist admissions tutors** in their search for the best students

THIS BOOK IS NOT:

- **a series of templates.** Obviously it would be extremely foolish as well as illegal to use any part of these personal statements, even if you 'move the language around a bit'

- **a set of perfect personal statements.** There is no such thing as a model personal statement. All of these are genuine personal statements, with strengths and weakness as varied as their writers. All of them have been successful, however, and the odd slip or error you will find in them should reassure you that mere mortals can apply and win offers

The Personal Statement's Importance

WHO READS IT?

Admissions tutors (or 'admissions officers') in the department to which you have applied will read them as they search to identify applicants who will have a genuine interest and a real ability in their subject area.

POPULAR COURSES

The personal statement can be absolutely crucial if you are applying to the most popular courses. You need a carefully considered and crafted personal statement to help you stand out from the crowd because:

- the competition is becoming fiercer
- most applicants will have top academic results and predictions
- most applicants will have strong references

In oversubscribed departments, admissions tutors are likely to go through personal statements with a fine-toothcomb.

Additionally, now that the reference is no longer confidential, admissions tutors regard the personal statement as possibly more valuable.

Queen Mary, University of London

The personal statement provides an important opportunity to differentiate yourself from the other applicants.

University of Cambridge

The personal statement is an applicant's opportunity to demonstrate their personal commitment and motivation to their subject which can never be shown by examination results alone.

Oxford University

The personal statement is the most important aspect of the UCAS form after a student's predicted grades.

Manchester University

To a certain extent, the statements selected for this book reflect the greater emphasis placed on the Personal Statement by those admissions tutors experiencing the greatest difficulty in distinguishing between large numbers of extremely capable candidates.

LESS POPULAR COURSES

Courses that are not so popular do not always place great emphasis on the personal statement, but there is no doubt that a good personal statement will help put you in control, and mean that you will be able to choose between institutions that are all keen to recruit you.

WHEN TO BEGIN

Start early and **apply before the official deadlines** (mid-October for Oxbridge, Medicine, Dentistry and Veterinary Science, and January 15th for other courses) because:

- admissions tutors start sorting through applications and making offers before the deadlines, so it is in your interests to apply while there is still a full complement of places

- admissions tutors read hundreds of forms and they often make an immediate decision. Applications that are received before the deadline have more time to be considered carefully

- early application suggests organisation and enthusiasm - an excellent impression to make

- early application means that you are lessening the admissions tutor's load that is heaviest during the mad rush just before the deadline. Your work will be appreciated and your application will enjoy the 'halo effect'.

HOW TO BEGIN

Sit down with masses of clean paper and brainstorm the suggestions for ingredients listed in the following two sections.

WHAT TO INCLUDE IN THE FIRST 60%

Your reasons for choosing this particular course, and your knowledge and experience of, as well as interest and capability in, the subject applied for.

Include relevant:

- books

- journals, periodicals, newspapers or magazines

- talks, public meetings

- courses and trips

- a project or coursework piece that you particularly enjoyed

- people: experts or professionals

- science documentaries or arts programmes

- visits (to universities, businesses etc)

- workshops, conferences

- placements, work experience
- gap year, secondment, summer school
- evening classes, clubs, adult education

Sound reasons for choosing the subject are normally the most important aspect of the statement.

Manchester University

How is your interest in the subject expressed outside the classroom?

University of Cambridge

Your personal statement is primarily an academic statement, and you must target it very directly towards the subject in which you are interested.

Durham University

Admissions tutors are always impressed by applicants who have 'breadth'. Try to show that you have an appreciation of current affairs in your field.

Queen Mary, University of London

WHAT TO INCLUDE IN THE REST

Activities and positions (see A below) that have developed the general skills and qualities (see B below) that are valuable to **all** students who study **any** subject. These differ from the skills **specifically** required for your subject that you covered in the first 60%.

(A) Examples of activities and positions:

- work experience, including work shadowing
- positions of responsibility
- contributions to the community at school, home or elsewhere
- sports
- hobbies
- time spent abroad or travelling
- worthwhile gap year plans if applying for deferred entry

(B) Examples of skills and qualities developed and demonstrated:

- communication
- numeracy
- problem solving
- listening
- responsibility
- team working and response to supervision
- organisation and time management
- initiative
- willingness to learn
- self-discipline
- commitment
- patience
- stamina
- leadership
- confidence
- sensitivity

Note well: you will not be able to include all of these achievements and ideas, so only pick your personal Olympic Gold Medals to describe in detail.

A long list of everything you have done is much less impressive than picking one or two things and writing about the skills you learned from them.

Durham University

The personal statement is the best way for students to prove that they are well-rounded individuals by discussing any involvement with clubs, societies, part-time employment, volunteering etc.

University of Leicester

HOW MUCH TO WRITE

- The electronic application form gives you room for approximately a side of A4 paper (about 500 words or **4,000 characters including spaces**).

- If you really want to irritate hard-pressed admissions tutors by wasting their time, you will waffle and repeat yourself.

- On the other hand you must not squander this chance to impress them by displaying your enthusiasm and knowledge in as much detail as you can. Be sure not to short-change yourself by writing more briefly than you need to if you have important things to say.

 Avoid writing something which is very short as this suggests a lack of attention.

University of Leicester

BLOWING YOUR OWN TRUMPET

- Remember that **self praise is no praise**. Not only can it sound arrogant, but it is less powerful than when it comes from others.

- Remind your referee that at some activity you are or have been remarkable, and it is a true and worthwhile achievement, it can be written into your reference. You could well write your referee a list of points for possible inclusion in the reference, and if the list is presented politely as a series of suggestions (rather than a set of demands) they will be delighted to have some of the hard work of researching and drafting a reference done for them.

HOW TO COMPOSE

Because **there is no spell-check facility on the UCAS form** you would be unwise to type the personal statement straight in, so compose a draft in Word and then copy and paste it into the application to see how much room you have to play with.

THE OPENING

Ideally this should be arresting and original. Easier said than done!

Consider:

1   describing the first time you realised that the subject was fascinating

2   using a relevant quotation

It is often recommended that you try to make your opening sentence stand out.

This can be effective - it is certainly better to be original than open with a cliché - but you need to be careful: you could come across as an oddball.

University of Cambridge

Write as you talk for as many pages as you like and somewhere in there you'll get a zingy little opening paragraph.

Brian Heap, 'Degree Course Offers'

THE END

The conclusion is the last impression you make upon the reader and psychologically is very powerful.

These three ways can end a personal statement effectively:

1   **summarise the whole personal statement** and assert that the writer is capable and keen. This gets the job done, and although it is not particularly creative most statements end this way

2   more creative and less repetitious writers may **use the conclusion as a springboard** for a new idea that grows logically and coherently from what has been stated in the personal statement

3   most satisfying and structurally impressive may be a circular structure to **echo the very start** of the personal statement and give the same idea a fresh direction or twist

WORDS TO AVOID

Psychologists and admissions experts at The University of Hertfordshire [reported by Education Guardian, 11th October 2005] have found that specific words and phrases can damage chances of acceptance.

As you can see, the top 10 words to exclude either sound **exaggerated** or **negative**:

always	fault
never	hate
nothing	mistake
awful	panic
bad	problems

REAL HOWLERS

Although a howler probably brightens up the admissions tutor's day almost as much as discovering an applicant with ability and motivation, you should not set out to entertain at your own expense! Here is a short list from the University of Glasgow's archive:

> *My ambitions include learning to sky dive, becoming fantastically rich as well as improving my A-Level grades.*

> *At school I held the position of head bog.*

> *I'm training a pet rat and have recently become interested in reading.*

> *I also enjoy driving, especially off the road.*

> *I have many interests, both interlectual and social.*

QUALITY CONTROL

To avoid amusing the admissions tutor inadvertently, make sure you **show your personal statement to two or three other people**. A subject teacher and a Higher Education and Careers teacher would be obvious choices, and they should make informed recommendations. However, **you ultimately must be the one to decide** what is included or omitted and how it is expressed; the material in the application is yours, which is why the statement is called *"personal"*.

THE TEN GOLDEN RULES

Follow these Golden Rules and you won't waste this chance for admissions tutors to form a favourable opinion of you.

To stand out from the crowd:

1. **research courses thoroughly** to show your enthusiasm for and understanding of the subject

2. **be specific** and display precise knowledge; don't be vague

3. **be honest**; only include what you know about so that you can't be caught out

4. try to **sound interesting and interested**, but don't overdo it and gush

5. **express your information and ideas clearly**

6. **don't be negative**; see failures as 'learning experiences'

7. **organise** your material

8. **don't state the obvious or repeat yourself**

9. **consider speeling, apostrophe's & grammer** (mistakes are irritating, or what?)

10. **don't mis-use words** in a vain attempt to look clever.

> *Don't lie, embroider or stretch the truth.*

University of Cambridge

THE PLATINUM RULE

is this:

DON'T TELL, SHOW

Rather than just **claiming** to be enthusiastic or informed about your subject, **demonstate** your interest and understanding by describing:

- the background to your interest in the subject
- ways in which you are currently following up this enthusiasm
- what exactly you know about the subject.

Don't just list what you did, tell us what you learnt from it.

Queen Mary, University of London

Read the openings to the following two personal statements and judge which applicant to an engineering course is better.

Ask yourself which applicant:

1. displays the most convincing enthusiasm

2. demonstrates the most genuine knowledge

3. is less likely to drop out

4. is more likely to be hardworking and gain a top class degree?

Applicant A

I have always wanted to study engineering and I have a huge passion for the subject. I have never enjoyed the arts subjects, so I feel that my future lies with the sciences. I enjoy Maths and Physics A-Levels greatly, I am very quick with numbers and I relish the challenge of formulae and equations. I feel my gifts in these subjects will help me when I get to university and later when I have won my qualification to work as an engineering professional.

I am very good with people, and have made a very successful prefect. An excellent sportsman, I have always participated two hundred percent in every team I have played for. Although I hate going to the theatre whenever the school has taken me, I love great films, especially war ones where weapons and buildings are important, so I know I'd make a good engineer. Otherwise I am as keen on socialising as any other teenager of my generation! I much in demand as a 'DJ' at parties. I intend to subsidise my time at university by earning money through this love of mine, and in my gap year I am planning to spend most of the time in Thailand, which I here is a beautiful country that has many beach parties. Hopefully my DJ skills can come in useful there before I come and settle down to my studying engineering at your university!

Applicant B

As a child, I was inquisitive and liked to see how everything worked, often dismantling objects beyond repair in my quest for this knowledge. This process of investigation, discovering, learning and rebuilding continued through Lego until I discovered Design Technology. Through this subject, I have found ways to express myself through the various design problems that I have been faced with. It was through DT, and a trip to the design museum in London, that I discovered Marc Newson, an Australian designer/architect, whose combinations of clean materials and natural/organic shapes really inspired me when commencing a coat hook as a design project, and I have now started designing a lectern for a Tudor building using various source books to aid me. I am also in the process of completing a physics paper on the engineering of boat hulls and how this affects their speed, an area that appeals to me, as I am a keen sailor.

Whilst concerned with aesthetics of shape and form, it is how the structures work within the product, both physically and mechanically, that really interests me. In the Lower Sixth, I attended a science symposium, with seminars on engineering at university; these broadened my understanding of the nature of the subject at university. I also managed to talk with an engineering student about life at university and what it entails. During the previous summer holiday, I spent a day at City University, being shown round their engineering facilities and getting a taste for the different types of engineering available. These events gave me a good insight into what exactly engineering is about and fuelled my interest to study an engineering based course at university, as I can see myself enjoying the challenge of the projects which were being completed.

THE VERDICT

Although Candidate A is certainly direct and may well be honest, the personal statement is far less impressive than Candidate B's because it:

- tells rather than shows
- offers little or no evidence for the claims that are made
- does not talk about the course enough
- forgets that self-praise is no praise.

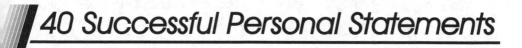

40 Successful Personal Statements

Historical debate can be applied to almost every aspect of the past; no situation is black and white, there is always a grey area to be exploited by an unconventional opinion, as portrayed in many of the extra history sessions I have attended. For example a South African speaker projected a novel point of view regarding the history of the battle of 'Rourke's Drift' last year.

Studying English and History A-levels, I have encountered many conflicting and ambitiously alternative beliefs to the true course of events, the Bayeux tapestry illustrates this in that the Norman knights dominate the source, though this level of superiority for one faction is highly unlikely given other evidence. By studying medieval history for the past year, with its limited resources I have enjoyed developing skills of analysing and evaluating sources. This also has been an essential ability for my investigation into the life of Saladin, which draws strongly on these skills as the Eastern writers vary greatly in opinion from the Western attitude of the time. Eastern sources, for example, portray their general, Saladin, as being of a far superior standard militarily to Richard the Lionheart, which in reality is a very debatable assertion. One of the most enjoyable aspects of English is watching the plays we study enacted on stage, for example 'Hamlet' at the Old Vic, which can offer alternative ways to interpret a text; one example is the relationship between Hamlet and Gertrude which can be exploited to suit the director, this objective perspective is often useful for interpreting a historical source. I feel this type of exposure is essential to fully comprehending the ancient literature a course in History would involve.

> *Some nice historical material here, but it would have been stronger if the novel point of view of the South African speaker had been precisely described, along with the 'other evidence' that suggests the Normans weren't so superior, the reason why Saladin's superiority is debatable, and the kinds of relationship possible between Gertrude and Hamlet.*

It is the unknown that makes Ancient History so significant, nothing is certain, and so there is always room for individual opinion and debate. I feel my other two A-levels, Physics and Mathematics have helped this, developing my historical analysis in a more direct and focussed way. In Physics, I recently researched a great scientific debate regarding 'Schrodinger's Cat', a historic change from the basic laws of Classical physics, set up by the renowned Isaac Newton, to laws of Quantum Mechanics, where nothing is certain, a topic still under a great deal of scrutiny and dispute.

Good, precise relation of other subjects to Ancient History.

As Captain of Debating in house, I have experienced the importance of individual opinions and diverse views that are all essential to a final outcome. Having completed a week of work experience with a QC in Winchester, the argument and debate of justice highlights the relevance of understanding and exploiting all the sources available. To this end wider reading has always been of great relevance for all of my subjects, and so I have indulged both in titles of scientific importance, such as 'Mr. Tompkins In Paperback', a book introducing and expanding on the theory of relativity, and those of more literary consequence, for example 'Heart of Darkness' (Joseph Conrad) or 'Midnight's Children' (Salman Rushdie), both of which write with a colonial, and so historical, perspective.

I have almost completed my Gold Duke of Edinburgh Award, after undertaking a World Challenge expedition to Honduras in 2003. £200 of the funds I raised for the trip, through working for two weeks in an institute for disabled children, I donated to the school towards the sensory room they were developing. Encouraged by contributing in this way, I volunteered to spend my Wednesday afternoons at 'Brimble Hill', another such institution for the following year. In addition to being part of a group helping to build a house for a poverty stricken couple, whose home was destroyed by Hurricane Mitch, I traversed the country's highest mountain of 2500m over a period of 5 days, carrying a 22 kilo rucksack containing tent, supplies and other equipment. This sort of experience, apart from developing my endurance, also contributes to my interest in the third world and their history; as well as the history that has pushed countries like ours into such a successful and prosperous present.

Nice descriptions of life outside the classroom and beyond the syllabus demonstrate independence, and the writer ends with evidence of an inquiring mind.

Offers from:
Durham, Edinburgh, Exeter, Leeds, St Andrews

Social anthropology is the main course I am interested in studying because, it seems, it would suit my interests in the subjects that I am studying at the moment and my outside interests. I enjoy travelling and experiencing different cultures (this summer I went to Namibia where I met a Bush tribe called the Himba) yet I constantly find myself embarrassed at my lack of understanding at the difference between other peoples' worlds and our own. It seems Social Anthropology challenges us to rid ourselves of the preconception bred into us by western society and opens our eyes to a different view. I would like to learn about these different views of the world - why the way things are in our present world and if there is an answer in the past to our current situations socially. What makes our modern society tick, action and reaction? In Coetzee's book 'Waiting for the barbarians' the administrator uncovers the remains of an ancient civilisation which helps lead him to questions about the sheltered and blinkered world in which he lives. I believe this is, although slightly cliche, a good example of perhaps what I would hope to experience in studying the subject at University.

> *Some good awareness of what the subjects involve. More specific detail on the Himba tribe (how does their society differ from ours, precisely?) and less on the very general musings about modern society would have improved this opening.*

At the moment I study Medieval history and History of Art both of which look at the past; in history, the life of government, war and the reasons for events happening. I am doing my Coursework on Saladin and his role as the champion of Islam in the 12th century. Part of the study requires the examination of the difference (and similarities of western Christians and eastern Moslem), an interesting anthropological angle. And in History of Art the remains of what past civilisations have left (such as the Greeks and Romans), the Renaissance and 20th century art. In Art I am currently conducting a personal investigation into the work of Henry Moore and Barbara Hepworth, two leading British sculptors of the early 20th century. Interestingly much of their influence for creating the simplified, almost abstract human figures was from the influence of primitive culture's art, this is mostly African tribal pieces. This shows how our modern society can learn from other cultures even if at the time they were labelled as Primitive and Savage. I also go to weekly life drawing classes as I find this helps my skills in art and is good fun.

Aspects of current academic study are well linked to Anthropology and Sociology.

As far as other extra-curricular activities go I am a keen sportsman and have played rugby at various levels since I was nine, this includes representing Yorkshire, my local town club and the First Team at school. I have competed in athletics for Yorkshire as well (throwing the javelin and long jump). I also like playing squash, football and surfing. At school we participate in weekly community projects and I have worked in an old people's home, looked after primary school children (a testing experience!) and done environment work (litter picking).

In my year off I plan to work on the Lord Nelson (a Tall Ship designed for the disabled) for a period of two weeks at sea, initially. I hope this will be an enjoyable but also enlightening experience as I will be helping the disabled do something they would not usually experience in our protective, smothering western culture: danger. After this I plan then to travel to France to work in Riems, learning French and gaining work experience and money for later trips.

The catalogue of extracurricular commitments starts with some impressive achievements, but the reference to litter picking seems to be scraping the barrel and could well have been omitted. Ends nicely and appropriately with a final mention of society's treatment of the people with disabilities.

Offers from:
Durham, East Anglia, School of Oriental and African Studies, Sussex

Architecture

Nearly all that I have an interest in or work towards involves architecture. I have long been inspired by the works of Friedensteich Hundertwasser. What attracts me to his work is his use of colour, which he has translated nimbly into his architecture. I admire the way he has been able to construct edifices which blend nature, fairytale and sculpture. However, I have often wondered whether his creations are inhabitable. To me the most interesting part of architecture is fusing beauty with practicality. This interest drew me to do work experience in Philip Starck's St Martins Lane Hotel in London. I walked in for the first day of work and I was completely mesmerised. The way Starck has converted an old office block is so efficient; instead of hiding this fact he has celebrated it, using the nature of the building to his advantage. He has resourcefully kept the very metropolitan like office ambience to the hotel and it is this that makes it completely iconoclastic. I was excited to hear that Stark is building a new hotel in Buenos Aires Argentina, as I wonder how he was going to manage with the unadventurous architecture department of South America.

Mentions of specific architects and their works display both interest and knowledge impressively.

Recently my family has taken on the project of building an Argentine house. Wanting to make the house environmentally friendly, we searched the country high and low for solar panels and wind turbines. There was a sufficient lack of trading in this department, which I found appalling. My aspiration is to promote the uses of alternative energy in South America. Through learning architecture I could come to understand how these can be incorporated into buildings. My interest in eco friendly housing and resourcefulness in architecture, introduced me to the works of Alex McKaley. Unable to build higher than 6 foot on a site in London, he built downwards. His initiative and problem solving in this piece is remarkable. To give natural light to the house he has constructed glass 'light tubes' which plummet through the floors of the house, flooding light into the deepest floors of the house.

Motivated by McKaley's ingenuity I have taken up set design. So far I have managed to devise a design for a school production: Lorca's 'Yerma'. The process was very rewarding. It taught me to think deeper into a play and also how to go about making maquettes of the sets- using scale and a range of materials. I was inspired to do this by the set design of an earlier production of Antigone- an impressive temple facade. This coincidentally led me to take up Classical Civilisation, which by studying I have been opened to the world of ancient architecture. In the Easter holidays I am embarking on a trip to Greece. There I will be able to piece together the friezes and the metopes of the Parthenon, which I have seen, to the sheer scale and structure of the remains. I have come to appreciate the beauty of early classical architecture, understanding that there are many well thought-out elements which come together to create the colossal body. At my school I have been taking part in a group that puts on exhibitions of our work and recently have been designing a mural for a piece of public art. I have also been taking part in photography lessons, learning the bizarre ways in which chemicals can create art; and life drawing classes, which has helped me with accuracy and structure in my own paintings and carpentry, developing my creative 3D skills.

I appreciate that architecture is a subject that needs commitment and dedication; I feel that I have these qualities. I meet deadlines in my work, this my teachers will support. I am a house captain and head of sport, which involves organising others, raising teams and rallying support, as did my past position as head of lower school. Through this I have learnt to take responsibility for myself and others. I have also successfully completed my trident award involving work experience, a course of horse whispering with Martin Harduoy and the upkeep of a school library, again exercising my organisation.

> *Much excellent demonstration of enthusiasm for and awareness about architecture both ancient and modern, and an appropriate emphasis on artistic skills.*

Offers from:
Liverpool, Manchester, Newcastle, Sheffield

Architecture

For many years I have had a unique perception of my surroundings, always interested in the details and possibilities of the buildings I view. My passion for architecture has been fuelled both by experiences within my design orientated upbringing and by personal exploration.

In my AS personal investigation Art has allowed me to explore a range of talented architects and artists. This has helped to expand my creative knowledge and perception of my surroundings as well as also spur interest in the likes of 'Aldo Rossi' and my favorite 'Daniel Libeskind' who I intend to focus my A level personal study around. I took a huge interest in his drawing techniques especially the 'micromegas,' which combine space with intricate detail in a structural form. Aldo Rossi impressed me for his theory of architecture and his great range of articles, including his structural sketches which are eye opening. I hope to investigate a wider range of architects when studying for my degree. I have enjoyed reading books on the likes of Frank Lloyd Wright, one of the great pioneers of modern architecture, and I intend to visit the Guggenheim he built in New York. I have already visited the Guggenheim in Bilbao by Frank O Gehry, an incredible building. I feel it is just as important to observe and study images of structure and design from all aspects as it is to read about the history and current standing architecture, in order to develop a wide as possible foundation to work from. I have a good understanding of the discipline and motivation it takes to become and practice as an architect, and I believe enthusiasm and genuine interest is the best and most reliable form of motivation.

> After the writer's throat has been cleared in the first sentence with a claim to uniqueness that is not explained and might seem arrogant, the personal statement improves by displaying some precise knowledge about and clear enthusiasm for Architecture.

I have particularly enjoyed studying my more specific subjects in the Sixth Form however studying Classical Civilization for GCSE really helped me appreciate Classical and Hellenistic architecture, in particular The Parthenon which I have studied in great detail. I am fascinated by the history of architecture and the stages it has passed through, and if presented with the opportunity I would like to pursue that interest during my degree.

> Good idea to turn other academic subjects to Architecture, but it is not really made to count. More detail on the Parthenon would have been telling.

Work experience has been an integral part in developing my interest in architecture. As well as working on building sites, I have been lucky enough to work in a major architects firm, Hamilton Associates, in London and with a Structural Engineer who kindly taught me the basics of CAD. Although I appreciate the vital importance of drawing, this experience contributed to my desire to become fully accomplished in 3D Computing Design and CAD. This added to my understanding of what the course and career involves and how perception, attention to detail and development of visual skills are so important. I have also always liked the challenge of constructing small buildings myself with limited resources, such as log sheds and car ports. These small projects have helped me develop basic practical skills.

> *Work experience is clearly appropriate and has given some useful insights into the practice of Architecture, as has some hands-on experience of putting up basic structures.*

I have enjoyed communicating well with people; frequent holiday work in a restaurant has contributed to this also training as a swimming coach has taught me the reward that can be gained teaching those younger than me. In the Combined Cadet Force I reached the rank of Corporal, in which I learnt leadership skills and to speak effectively in public. Being House Prefect and helping in the production of the House play has taught me to plan ahead and organize people. I know it is important for an architect to be able to communicate well with a wide selection of people, and I feel I can convey my ideas clearly to people as well as understand others.

I believe that training as an architect, even though the course is very specific, would help me to develop a broad range of skills that can be built upon throughout life.

> *The final sentence is waffly, but the key skills described before it are important.*

Offers from:
Edinburgh College of Art, Leeds Metropolitan, Manchester, Newcastle, Oxford Brookes

I have had a long founded interest in History of Art with a particular interest in both the modern Parisian art world and the Renaissance period. I enjoyed the Personal Study component of my A level course, which developed my essay writing skills, such as researching sources and being selective about the material used. On the modern aspect of History of Art, I have enjoyed Matisse, and admired how he endured poverty and yet was able, through his unique works with expressive and inventive use of colour, to establish himself in the Parisian art world. I find it interesting that suffering and adversity is so often associated with genius. I also loved his more primitive pieces, where he floods the viewer with colour, while figures seem to float on top of the canvases. History of Art offers me the ability to satisfy not only an interest in the past, but also an opportunity to study artistic development. I have enjoyed studying the lives of artists and sculptors as well as the development in artistic techniques and the influence of different cultures such as the Byzantine on the Renaissance, and Moorish and Islamic qualities on the late works of Matisse.

Begins with a fitting list of artists. Mentions of interesting details of specific works would have made the writer's interest more apparent.

One of my favourite Renaissance periods was the 1420's in Florence, which saw a meeting between the late Gothic International style (Gentile de Fabriano) and a new approach based on naturalism rooted in the study of proportion, perspective and classical art. The leading practioner of this new art was Masaccio whose death presented the next generation of artists (Fra Angelico) with the freedom to integrate the two stylistic trends in their own fashion.

More detail makes this a stronger paragraph. Some knowledge of the subject beyond the syllabus would have been impressive, too.

I enjoy writing and compiling essays, analysing material and using it to argue a point of view. This was the side of my Geography course that I enjoyed the most. It has allowed me to develop presentational skills that should prove useful in the future.

Beyond my studies I enjoy a wide range of sports and I represented my school at first team level at rugby, hockey, tennis and rackets, the last two of which I was captain. I have played representative rugby at County level and won the player of the tour award while touring with the school XV. I have enjoyed the team aspects of playing sport and I have had to adopt a disciplined approach to fulfilling all my sporting and academic commitments.

Within my house at school I was a prefect and had a responsibility for day to day routines within the house. I also spent time last summer raising money for the Teenage Cancer Trust by cycling with a friend on a tandem on a 120 mile trip from school to my home in Sussex.

I have organised a busy Gap year that will involve some work initially as a shop assistant and most recently as an office helper in an insurance company to raise funds for travel in Australia and New Zealand.

Some good key skills that demonstrate commitment and organisation that will be useful.

The claims about the enjoyment of writing and debating in Geography are too vague to cut much ice.

During the year I am also attending an art history course. This will involve tuition in art, history, architecture and literature and travel throughout Italy including Venice, Florence, Siena and Rome. I am especially looking forward to visiting Rome and the Vatican Museums and seeing Michelangelo's masterpiece, The Last Judgement in the Sistine Chapel, as well as the frescoes by Raphael. I am also looking forward to visiting the Uffizi in Florence, to study some of my favourite artists of the Renaissance period. My visit to Italy will broaden my interest and love for the subject, as viewing the works first hand brings the subject to life. I hope that the work and travel during my Gap year will further develop my self reliance and thus help prepare me for life at university.

Plans to further knowledge of the subject in this way are helpful because they indicate interest.

Offers from:
Leeds, Nottingham, Oxford Brookes

A combined course would provide me with a breadth of study in the three interrelated subjects that I find most intellectually inspiring: Politics, Theology and History of Art.

Since Tony Blair's overwhelming victory in 1997, I have followed political development with zeal. Being a regular subscriber to Politics Review has given me knowledge to broaden my opinions and tackle contemporary political debates. I have heard speakers like Michael Ancram, my local MP, and Michael Hart, an expert on psephology, and this has given me first hand contact with experts which I have found stimulating because of the necessity for spontaneous answers to the questions posed by the audience. As for further reading, I have enjoyed "After Blair - Conservatism beyond Thatcher" by Kieron O'Hara, and as it is important for me to cross-reference between subjects, I have read "From Plato to NATO", a selection of essays by different authors on a selection of great philosophers including Marx, J.S.Mill and Rousseau.

Some excellent names are dropped into the paragraph but it's a little vague. Interesting ideas that the politicians and authors expressed would have been impressive.

The great ethical debate between a fundamentally humanistic view and the contradictory theistic religious world view has for centuries divided man to lesser or greater degrees and fascinates me. However, to suggest that Theology is merely the study of the confrontation between the religious and the non-religious would be underestimating it. I enjoy the sociological, anthropological and linguistic sides to the subject to as illustrated in "You wretched Corinthians" by Hans Fror which is a reconstruction of the extensive Corinthian correspondence between Paul and the church at Corinth and aptly portrays relationships in the Early Church in a light-hearted and imaginative way.

More detailed description of reading makes this a strong paragraph.

I have enjoyed partaking in heated discussions that invariably occur at our Philosophy and Theology clubs and I appreciate that listening and approaching the potentially sensitive subject with an open mind is essential.

An example of two of the discussions would have spoken volumes.

I discovered my fascination with colour, method and structure in paintings the art library. I have sound knowledge of a range of artists from Toulouse-Lautrec to Basquiat from studying art to A-level and now endeavour to make my sound knowledge comprehensive. I visit the National Gallery and the Tate Modern on a regular basis, and on a recent visit, I was fascinated by Chris Ofili's exhibition entitled The Upper Room, not only aesthetically, but also because of its religious and political framework. Consequently, I have chosen to base my personal study on him.

At another exhibition to see the key impressionists Turner, Whistler and Monet was astounding. In February, I had the equally incredible experience of seeing The Gates, a piece of installation art by Jean-Claude and Christo in Central Park, New York. It was a spectacular sight and one I am privileged to have seen first hand.

Enthusiasm is clear here. Ofili's religious and political framework could have been briefly described, and quite what was outstanding about the impressionists and incredible about The Gates remains vague.

As for my extra curricular pursuits, I have been appointed Cultural Representative in my house which involves me raising awareness amongst my peers for artistic opportunities. Having supported Amnesty International for over six years, I was pleased to be appointed Head of Charities last year. All of this, combined with being a house prefect, teaching children with varying degrees of disabilities and participating in numerous house events has taught me valuable communication, toleration and leadership skills.

This brief description of other activities and interests that involve the use and acquisition of key skills is good.

Offers from:
Birmingham, Durham, Glasgow, Leeds, Queen's Belfast

Arts - Combined (Music and Philosophy)

When Socrates asked how should a man live I think he was really questioning the key to the significance of human existence. The ideas of a God and of morality intrigue me and by studying philosophy, I expect to have my ideas challenged and expanded. After reading 'The Story of Philosophy' by Brian Magee, which was a simple but very interesting introduction to the great philosophers, I found myself drawn to Kant. His deontological theory caught my eye and his argument, that we gain knowledge through both experience and understanding, particularly interested me. This then led me to read 'German Philosophers' which contained a particularly pertinent analysis of Kant's theories by Roger Scruton. He presents Kant's thoughts through modern idioms, while presupposing the least possible knowledge of philosophy which I found to be fascinating. Kant's thoughts are challenging, and for a project I decided to write an essay on the strengths and weaknesses of Kant's theories. My interest in philosophy was strengthened by a talk given by Michel Lacewing. He spoke of the differences and similarities between knowledge and wisdom. This led me to think of the origins of wisdom, and how it develops throughout one's life, and it is from this that my interest in meta-ethics stems. The question of morality and how it is a function of one's culture and upbringing is fascinating to me; are you born wise or does wisdom develop throughout your life? This question of intrinsic values is one I am eager to do more research on in the future. The study of Philosophy will, I believe, offer opportunities to become an increasingly independent thinker, and it will demand of me not only curiosity but the willingness to hear other opinions as well as developing my own.

> *Some excellent wide reading is detailed here, demonstrating the fitting spirit of inquiry, and the talk that is mentioned was clearly an inspiring and provocative experience.*

I set myself high standards, and have done so from an early age, exemplified by my achievement of a distinction at Grade VIII violin whilst under the pressure of GCSE examinations. I began learning the violin under the Suzuki method and between the ages of 5 and 16 I was a member of a group of violinists. We regularly gave concerts, including one in Buckingham Palace, and from this my passion for performing began. We toured Hungary in 2000 playing in monasteries, concert halls, music schools and embassies. As a result of our successes, we travelled around the USA to much acclaim. In the summer of next year I will complete my Trinity Violin Diploma. My main work will be the Schumann Sonata Op.105 which I will also use for my

A2 recital. For this I am concentrating solely on the Romantic period playing pieces by Svendsen and Wieniawski.

In my A2 studies of set works for history and analysis I have been enlightened by the knowledge of changing styles in composition which have lead to a much greater intensity in my playing. In my study of Wagner's 'Tristan and Isolde' I discovered Schopenhauer, who believed it was through the arts, particularly through music, that human beings find release from the pain of existence. Through music we can enjoy the experience of being out of space and time.

Despite the rules of Serialism, I have found composing within this genre an equally liberating practice, aided by my ability to play the piano at a Grade VI standard.

I have been a dedicated leader of both the Symphony and Chamber orchestras, the Chapel and Chamber choir and an award winning piano quintet, which all require dedication, diligence and a high standard of playing and singing. I have had additional responsibilities as a House Prefect entrusted with the pastoral care of a house of some 65 individuals of very differing character. I am keen to move forward and start the next stage of my education in which I can finally concentrate on those areas that both fascinate me intellectually and develop my passion for music; that, to me, is something to really look forward to.

> *Enthusiasm in performance and for academic study are catalogued in impressive detail.*

Offers from:
Durham, Edinburgh, Leeds, Newcastle, Nottingham, Oxford Brookes

I would like to study Biology because ever since I was young I have been interested in the way organisms work. From the age's of three to eleven I lived on a farm and this sparked questions about the behaviour and physiology of animals. I recently attended a seminar on the reintroduction of the Great Bustard to Britain. I found this particularly interesting due to the relevance it has towards me, as a person who lives in the vicinity of Salisbury. I also read the "Biological Sciences Review" which I find very interesting. I have also read a book on ecology by Paul Colinvaux called "Why Big Fierce Animals Are Rare", which interested me thoroughly, because it brought out a lot of points about how animals have evolved to fit their habitats. This has certified that the thing that really attracts me to Biology is the variety of animal life, particularly how animals evolve to cope with their natural habitat, their differences and yet at the same time their similarities.

> *The writer begins strongly by describing the starting point of the enthusiasm for the subjects that are applied for.*
>
> *Good examples demonstrate interest in the subject nicely, although something should have been made of 'Biological Sciences Review' to prove how the periodical is found interesting.*

I enjoyed the AS course very much, especially studying the human respiratory system and the heart, both of which have encouraged me to learn more. I think it is interesting how the body has evolved to be so perfect e.g. particularly adaptations of alveoli and blood capillaries to maximise efficiency of gas exchange. The way cells work is also of particular interest to me, looking at how enzymes are made and how they are transported. I have enjoyed studying DNA replication, and how it is done semi-conservatively and how precise editing mechanisms reduce the chances of mistakes. For my A2 course I am looking forward to learning more about human physiology. At university I hope to study more about invertebrate zoology.

> *Specific areas of the syllabus are detailed well here, suggesting enthusiasm.*

I have very much enjoyed playing sport, particularly rugby. I play flanker for the 3rd XV and represent the school at cricket and the house at football. As well as being keen on my sport, I have directed and acted in the house play, which was enjoyed by both audience and cast. This helped to develop my leadership and people management skills, as I had to direct people between the ages of 13 and 17. I also had to organise all aspects of the play including props, lighting and music which proved quite complicated.

In addition I am a House Prefect, which means I must be responsible enough to look after the younger years, and to be looked up to by setting a good example and at the same time being approachable. I work at my local Cancer Research shop, and have developed my people skills here too, by interacting with members of the public. I am also charity representative for the house which involves promoting awareness of the needs of others. Lately I have been working on sponsoring a child in Kenya. I have a European Computer Driving Licence, and have worked with computers all my life as my father is an IT teacher. My rank of Lance Corporal in the CCF has given me leadership and teamwork experience, as well as a sense of independence which I am sure will stand me in good stead for the next phase of my education.

Extracurricular activities that developed key skills are usefully catalogued.

Offers from:
Aberyswyth, Bangor, Leeds, Reading, St Andrew's

Business Studies/Business Management

My interest in the world of business has existed since an early age; however it was a talk by Sir John Harvey Jones which really inspired me. He emphasised the importance of people within business and of motivating them to succeed and to reach their maximum potential. A talk by Lord MacLaurin furthered this interest. He explained how Vodafone, founded in 1984 became one of the largest companies in the world, with a market capitalisation of £94 billion. He focused on the key components to success, the motivating of staff and successful marketing.

This excellent opening gives the origins of the interest in studying the subject.

I have completed work experience at the financial firm PKF, where I assisted in the auditing of a company's accounts and in the preparation of their annual reports. I carried out many tasks, including the checking of VAT payments and analysis of turnover and expenses. It was a very gratifying experience, because I was given all hands-on tasks, reporting to the Head of Department at the end of each day. It gave me a deeper understanding of the accounting side of a business, to complement my reading. I have also kept upto date with current economic events and market conditions and have a particular interest in the emergence of China as an economic giant.

Work experience is nicely appropriate here. The mention of China hints at an awareness of current business affairs, but it would have been an even stronger element if it had been more specific.

I have greatly enjoyed the Business Studies course at A-level. However, it was the Marketing section that particularly captivated me. The way in which a product is sold successfully is fascinating and, of course, fundamental to its success. It is striking to see how great an effect a successful marketing campaign can have on a business. This was something particularly stressed by Lord MacLaurin about Vodafone. He stated it was central to Vodafone's strategy, and explained that although sponsoring the Ferrari F1 team cost them £60 million a year, it generated world-wide exposure to an audience that would be suited to the company's services.

As with Harvey Jones in the opening paragraph, the writer is impressively willing to go into detail here.

I feel that my interests and my A-Level subjects are particularly suited to a degree in Business Studies. The analytical skills acquired in History and the awareness created by Politics, both in terms of current issues and in economic policy (such as Keynesianism and Monetarism), are relevant to the wider world of business.

As a House Prefect and Charity Representative I have had opportunities to develop leadership qualities. These have been enhanced further by my participation in the school teams for rugby, fencing and athletics. My participation as part of these teams has strengthened my skills in helping to motivate those around me. I have attended several Swansea Business Club meetings where guest speakers have included Dyfrig John (Deputy Chief Executive HSBC). I have also worked in the college archives. Last year I gained my Trident Gold award and the ECDL qualification.

With the help if my brother I have set up a Limited company which I ran during the holidays. This specialised in online retailing, with a fully automated website where customers placed their orders. I dealt with the day to day operational running of the company, which gave me good experience of both Customer Service and the management of a business. I enjoyed the challenges, such as controlling the cashflow and marketing the products.

In order to broaden my experience, I am planning a placement over the summer working with Halifax estate agents. This will give me an insight into the world of both Commercial and Residential property sales and valuations. This is a market of particular interest at the moment due to the uncertainty with house prices and the low buy-to-let returns. This will provide me with a further insight into the world of business and help to prepare me for the experience provided by higher education.

> *Other A level subjects and extracurricular activities are usefully listed with reference to key skills acquired or their relevance to business.*

Offers from:
Birmingham, Cardiff, Exeter, Manchester, York

The business world has fascinated me for a long time, triggered by following the fortunes of specific companies through the Economist and Financial Times. For example the international mining company Xstata whose expansion and diversification into various aspects of the mining sector produced rapid growth over the past three years. In contrast, Transiberian Gold, a company in the same sector, lacked the resources and initiatives to diversify away from precious metals and as a result has suffered decline. I am intrigued by the economic, geographical and managerial factors that influenced two such differing outcomes and my interest in such matters is the foundation for my choosing business studies. The influence of differing business concepts also interests me greatly, from the benefits of kaizen groups, to the greater efficiency of just in time management, or the cost implications gained from economies of scale, something that Xstrata was clearly able to further exploit through its ever heightening expansion. An interest in such case histories led me to being awarded the school business studies prize.

 Very good, detailed justifications for the writer's claim to be fascinated, using an interesting case study.

Studying human geography has shown me the enormous impact that geographical position can have on the business and economic prosperity of different countries. Climate, natural resources and global geographical positioning are key factors. Japan is such an example with regard to its proximity to the Asian markets, while Southern African states have developed almost solely out of their natural resources of gold and diamonds. Human geography has also highlighted the importance of continual innovation and change. New ideas are necessary to keep pace in a competitive market such as tourism, while at the same time continuing to consolidate successful industries.

Politics has shown me the significance of stability for maintaining sustained business growth, whilst at the same time some change can be a great benefit to business because it prevents stagnating commercial environments. For example, the end of Socialist regimes in Russia and China where market forces had previously been ignored, led to rapid expansion of these economies. The arrival of Margaret Thatcher's Conservative party in 1979 however, heralded the start of what appeared to be a dramatic economic recovery in Britain.

 The relevance of other A Level subjects to Business Management is shown cleverly here.

I played an active role in school life. I was head of my boarding house and a school prefect. I represented my school for the first teams at hockey and tennis. As part of the schools social service programme I worked at a local school for seriously handicapped children and I was a member of the college CCF for the past four years. I coached the junior school tennis team and have been awarded my Trident gold award.

A good, brief selection of extracurricular activities.

I am taking a gap year in order to broaden my experiences. This autumn I have been taken on by Henderson fund managers for a three month internship. This should prove invaluable in giving me an insight into the workings of a large company in the financial sector as well as earning money that will fund the rest of the year. I am also planning to study Spanish to give me a basic knowledge of the language, before going to Chile in January with Operation Raleigh where I will be helping in the conservation of the local environment and caring for children in Patagonia. Following this I plan to visit Peru and Bolivia where I look forward to witnessing first hand how these countries differ so greatly to more developed nations, both culturally and commercially.

Finishes nicely with appropriate work experience and a reference to the course, after having illustrated key skills such as organisation and initiative.

Accepted by:
Edinburgh, Exeter, Newcastle

Chemistry

Chemistry has always appealed to me more than any other subject, as it seems not only to underpin many aspects of other scientific disciplines, but also many fundamental aspects of life. For example, the study of medicine and human biology relies on the understanding of chemical reactions, such as asymmetric synthesis, which is used to produce more of one enantiomer of a drug than another to reduce the risk of the other enantiomer causing problems, as was the case with thalidomide. The study of forces and microstructure in physics similarly relies on the knowledge of atoms and molecules, taught in chemistry. More importantly for me, however, is the satisfaction of knowing that almost everything in chemistry seems to make logical sense. I am aware of many reactions and processes being oversimplified at GCSE and A level chemistry but the fundamental theories behind it all make sense. I am eager to further explore the more detailed aspects too, such as anomalies and exceptions to the 'rules', and to find out what makes them so. For example, zinc doesn't follow all the 'rules' and trends of a transition metal, nor does aluminium conform to being a typical metal, having some non-metal properties, such as the ability to bond covalently. My study in both maths and physics helps enormously, in that maths helps me to understand the mathematical principles in chemistry such as mole calculations and bond enthalpies, as well as analysing results, and physics has helped me to understand more the forces and interactions between molecules based on charges and polarity.

 The reasons given for studying Chemistry are supported by some excellently informed detail.

While at school, I was always very involved in school life. I represented my school in athletics and was captain of rowing, which gave me the opportunity to improve my leadership skills and learn how to work with a team. I also obtained school colours for both sports which are awarded for commitment to each. I sang in the school choir for two years, have reached grade six standard in singing, piano and drama, and have taken part in many school drama productions, which have all helped me to develop both organisation and confidence within myself. I was also awarded school music honours, for commitment to the choir. I was a house prefect and also the house representative of the chapel, both of which involve pastoral work with younger members of the house and has made me more patient and tolerant of others. I was also part of the school Christian union and spent one afternoon a week during term time helping in a local primary school.

I have had work experience at the Health Protection Agency Porton Down, working with a group researching into a vaccine against the botulism neurotoxin, which gave me an insight into aspects of biochemistry as well as experience of basic lab techniques. I am currently on a gap year, which I am taking in order to broaden my experiences, in which I am planning to travel at some point during the year for a few months, to Africa or Europe, so that I can experience a different lifestyle and culture from my own before embarking on my degree course.

Energy and organisation are shown in a good number of extracurricular achievements, and the Chemistry-related work experience is particularly appropriate.

Accepted by:
Bath, Bristol, Southampton

A Classics course would offer me the chance to develop a wide range of academic skills, from the grammatical challenge of the Greek and Latin languages to the criticism of literary texts. I hope that my wide range of interests and achievements will prepare me for such a course.

I have especially enjoyed the opportunity to study the Homeric epics, The Iliad and The Odyssey. In the former I have examined and enjoyed in particular the domestic scenes away from the battlefield and have found Homer's ability to portray a humane world through the medium of war poetry remarkable. Having read Deryck Williams,' Aeneas and the Roman Hero, I have found intriguing the contrast of Aeneas' patriotic aspirations with Achilles' more selfish concern for personal honour. I have especially enjoyed hearing Dr. Efi Spentzou talk about redefining the epic hero in Virgil's Aeneid. Spentzou's references to the political and social state of Rome after the civil war motivated me to consider the reason behind Virgil's modification of Homer's Greek hero. Through studying Lysias's work, On the murder of Eratosthenes, I have developed an interest in his use of oratory and rhetoric which he conceals behind a shrewdly constructed speech emulating the character of his client. His reference to the Thesmophoria and the questions raised about the status of women in society have inspired my interest in the role of women in the classical world, leading me to read S. Pomery's Goddesses, Whores, Wives, and Slaves. Next year I hope to travel to Greece to experience ancient archaeology first hand and broaden my knowledge of the Classical world.

> *Excellent references to classical works and authors display good knowledge, and the mentions of modern speakers and critics show enthusiasm that has gone beyond the classroom. The writer does not just name-drop, but goes on to describe the moments and ideas that have been found fascinating.*

I have had continuous involvement in various musical ensembles as a violinist, developing both my teamwork and leadership to the extent of winning the school string quartet prize. Competing in a national schools' competition in netball and also achieving grade 8 piano and violin both with distinction shows my ability to honour commitments and cope with a wide range of demands, along with inherent self-discipline and independence. I was awarded a Trident Gold certificate for my continued commitment to both orchestra and netball together with a week of work experience in St. Richard's Hospital, a challenging and rewarding experience. As Head of Music in my boarding house I will be organising the house concert, which will test my organisational and directorial skills while, as a House Prefect, I am responsible for younger children, a task that requires patience and an ability to earn respect.

 Impressive list of extra-curricular achievements is linked to important key skills such as organisation.

During my Gap Year I hope to broaden my experiences and give something back through volunteer work in a developing country and I also intend to pursue a JACT Latin course where I look forward to expanding my understanding of Classics with study of the Roman world.

I am an avid reader of English Literature, and I think the analytical skills I have developed in studying English literature will be most beneficial for the literary criticism of ancient texts. I have also been awarded a prize for Religious Education and Distinctions for History and RE essays, showing my ability to analyse sources and argue coherently. Losing only two marks in the Spanish Reading and Writing paper and only one mark in AS Greek overall clearly demonstrates my excellent understanding of language. Being adept at Maths denotes my good logic, a quality I consider invaluable for the study of ancient languages. I hope that studying Classics at tertiary level will stretch and enable me to further test my diverse abilities.

Lack of space means that the writer needs to be superficial here if so many subjects are to be mentioned. The Distinctions and AS performance would have been better noted by the Referee, and the claim that the writer loves English Literature could then have been supported by references to texts and authors.

Accepted by:
Cambridge, Bristol, Durham, Edinburgh, Leeds, Newcastle

Classics

I find Classics absorbing; it is much more than just an academic subject for me. I appreciate that, whether it is our alphabet and language, history or politics, art or architecture, advocacy, Euclid and the development of mathematics (Newton's giants shoulders), so much is owed to the Classical World. School classics meetings and reading in my spare time, from Russell's History of Western Philosophy or populist histories such as Tom Holland's Rubicon, or going round the British Museum, whet my appetite to learn more. Linguistically, it provides both an intellectual challenge and an insight into the basis of our language. Pythagoras said "all things are numbers" but, from my limited knowledge, modern philosophy seems to focus more on the meaning and structure of language. How did humans develop such complex grammar and syntax. Is it an innate quality within us? I enjoy and take pride in translating to and from Latin and Greek and have fun speaking them - I twice won the Salisbury Schools' Latin and Greek Speaking competition. I find Classical literature stimulating as well as demanding; Sophocles, in particular, has provided me with great pleasure. I find the complex issues surrounding the workings of fate in plays such as Oedipus Tyrannos intriguing. The insights into moral and political issues and especially the 'polis v nomos' issues of the Antigone have also been of great interest to me. Reading Philoctetes provided an opportunity to explore some of Aristotle's ideas on what constitutes Tragedy. The theme of suffering seems to expose aspects of the author's own persona, such as his attitude towards the Gods, his attempts to reconcile them with the arbitrary suffering of humans and his attitude to contemporary sophistry through the machinations of Odysseus.

> *This gushes a little; better to imply rather than state how absorbing and stimulating the subject is found. Some promising references to classical works and authors, but specific details and examples would have made this more impressive.*

Studying History gave me a valuable insight into the evolution of our society and developed my analytical skills and essay writing. This background should assist my study of Ancient History. Chemistry AS took my understanding of the material world beyond basic GCSE science, which should help me to appreciate Natural Philosophy and the Classical thinkers' efforts to make sense of the material world.

Outside class, I love sport and represented my school at first team level in Hockey, Netball and Tennis. As a School Prefect and Head of House, positions which involved real responsibilities, I learnt the importance of communication, organisation and diplomacy. I took an active part in discussion societies, which taught me to marshal my thoughts and research thoroughly before venturing an opinion. I worked at school in a home for disabled children, which was both rewarding and humbling. I study the piano for pleasure and this has given me greater appreciation of all types of music. I worked at the History Channel, which introduced me to the disciplines of working in a commercial environment. I was required, inter alia, to write a review of the Queen of Sheba Exhibition at the British Museum, which was challenging and which found its way onto the website. A gap year will broaden my outlook through travel and fulfil a desire to learn Spanish, which I intend to do in Bolivia, after working on a rain forest project. I also intend to visit some Classical sites, starting in Rome.

I appreciate only too well that I have merely scratched the surface of the subject at school. I now wish to deepen my knowledge at university. To quote Waugh, I want to be able to 'do myself full justice on the subject of Pindar's Orphism', although Donna Tart's book Secret History suggests that I should avoid probing too deeply the Orphic Mysteries! I hope that my commitment to and love of Classics will endow me with sufficient skill to study this demanding but rewarding subject.

Many activities in and out of school are made to refer to Classics.

The reference to Donna Tartt's book shows an interesting sense of humour, but would have been more effective if the author's name had been spelled correctly.

Accepted by:
Bristol, Durham, Edinburgh, Exeter, Nottingham, Oxford

Ever since I can remember I have wanted to pursue a career in the medical field; an interest fed by the idea of interaction with a wide variety of people on a personal level and fuelled by my enthusiasm for the sciences.

 A rather ordinary series of vague claims. As often is the case, the second paragraph (below) would have made a stronger opening because it is directly relevant to the subject.

An experience directed my attention towards dentistry. Spending some time at a dentist's surgery to have root canal treatment last year provided me with an insight into the way in which a dental practice works. I was particularly impressed by the intimacy of the dentist/patient relationship. To further explore this field I volunteered as an assistant in Dr. A Scott's dental surgery for two weeks and was able to observe various dental procedures such as root canal treatments, which I saw from the other end of the drill, as well as X-rays, extractions, and cavity fillings. I was able to assist the dentist with simple tasks such as finding the patients' records before surgery and the sterilising of instruments learning the meticulous procedures involved. Most rewarding for me was the opportunity to come into contact with the patients whilst in the waiting room which showed me the need for empathy and discretion in such an environment. This experience encouraged me to go on to discover more about other aspects of the profession leading me to Orthodontistry. For a week this year I undertook an internship with two orthodontists at 'Tingrinners Club', and was fortunate enough to observe unusual procedures such as the fabrication of retainers and dental models. I have continued to pursue my interest by shadowing the dentists, as regularly as possible, at the local dental practice in my town in Berkshire.

An excellent series of experiences entirely appropriate to the course show the writer's interest in and knowledge of Dentistry in a much more convincing way than the first paragraph.

As Chapel Representative, House Prefect and Head of Year Nine, I am now enjoying the responsibilities and roles that come with having progressed to the top of the school. Living in a boarding house has taught me to cope with many different types of people. Outside my boarding house I captained the first tennis team for three years, as well as playing rugby, squash, athletics and basketball all to first team level. The experience of working in an environment under pressure, amongst highly capable individuals has proved invaluable. For relaxation I play the piano as well as listening to a wide range of music. I have a high level of hand-eye coordination and I am well aware of the need for manual dexterity in my chosen profession. Undertaking the Duke of Edinburgh Gold award has necessitated a continuous involvement in expeditions around the United Kingdom under strenuous conditions. This has brought home to me the importance of teamwork and strength of character, whatever the situation. I also provide a weekly childminding service for the teachers of my school which has enabled me to communicate with younger children on a one-to-one level.

This worthy paragraph on personal skills might well have been left until later, while the more directly course-related paragraphs below that link more obviously with the first paragraphs could have been promoted.

My subscription to Biological Sciences Review and Physics Review as well as my reading of New Scientist has further stimulated my interest in aspects of dentistry. Imaging techniques such as magnetic resonance imaging and positron emission tomography were amongst some of the articles I found particularly appealing; the way in which photographs can be taken of your brain and internal organs, without damage amazed me. My Physics project on silicone breast implants gave me a greater view into the world of prosthetics in relation to aesthetics and demonstrated how one's body reacts to the input of various materials, which is clearly related to dentistry. From my personal experiences I have learnt that dentists not only treat teeth and mouths, but also people. Dentistry cuts across age, culture and personality.

Impressive references to journals show interest and enthusiasm beyond the syllabus, and the ability to talk about articles in the journals shows that this is not just name-dropping, but that knowledge has been gained.

I am a hard worker and enjoy learning and am eager to not only broaden my knowledge of the subject, but also to apply acquired understanding and skills to help improve the quality of people's lives. I am under no illusions as to the degree of involvement that dentistry demands on a physical, intellectual and emotional level. The practice of science must be both compassionate and informed.

Offers from:
Birmingham, King's College London

My initial attraction to Economics stemmed from a talk I attended by Prof. P Minford on the current economic situation in the EU. This focused on the introduction of the ten new countries and their effects on subsidies and employment. I subsequently attended another fascinating meeting in which we discussed the work of John Maynard Keynes. This brought to my attention the importance of stimulation of employment. The sheer volatility of the economy astonished me and this led me to read Keynes' 'The General Theory'.

Detailed and interesting reasons for the writer's application indicate that real enthusiasm and knowledge are present. An excellent start.

In order to explore the subject further, I helped to create a Stock and Shares trading club based largely around the FTSE 100 and founded a Young Enterprise Company for which I am currently the Managing Director. These opportunities gave me the chance to explore the effects of the economy on a small firm and on the national and international market. Most useful, however, was the chance to see the effect of my management on the results of the Young Enterprise Company. My role was to draw the company together and combine the strengths of each department. Being responsible to the staff and shareholders made diplomacy and discretion mandatory.

Good initiative, and descriptions of appropriate experience.

I have enjoyed two weeks work experience in a law firm in Liverpool, focusing on corporate law. The filing and organisation of the Dyson versus Hoover case absorbed the majority of my time and the work was fascinating as I was given free access to all the firm's documents on the case. Looking into this case further, presenting me with the opportunity to develop my understanding on trademark and patent law. Last Christmas I was also presented with the chance to do some work for MacDonalds in Tokyo. This large multinational firm offered a different experience to the work in Liverpool. I learnt a great deal about foreign economic conditions as well as being able to compare the situations in both England and Japan, in particular the influence that the large corporations hold on the national economy and the government. I have also enjoyed two weeks of work experience at a law firm in Japan, during which I spent time working with the partners of the firm. This was largely in management of personnel.

Work experience placements are not just listed, but it is made clear how the writer benefited from them. Excellent.

I have worked for the school's newspaper and this has helped me to improve my writing skills along with my ability to present my point of view. My attendance and participation at numerous debates and workshops have aided my communication as well as allowing me to gain a further understanding of current affairs. I have represented the 1st XI for football as goalkeeper along with captaining my cricket and rugby teams. These leadership opportunities were immensely beneficial as they provided the occasion to listen to the views of others and build team-working amongst the group of players. I am the head of my boarding house and this has enabled me to develop my leadership skills, in particular communicating my goals and aims to others. I have taken part in charity work in the Philippines, in an orphanage and in setting up schoolhouses. These experiences acted as a real motivator, and I found the work in Manila a particularly gratifying experience. This community service work, together with my work experience, enabled me to obtain a Trident Gold Award.

Good key skills and initiative described in detail here.

During my gap year, I plan to secure a placement in the city of London to gain experience of the current economic situation in order to apply my reading to the national economy and compare this with past trends. This may present me with the opportunity to travel through Asia and Africa. During these travels I hope to not only improve my understanding of the cultures of the places I visit, but also the current economic problems that many face.

Worthwhile plans are nicely appropriate to Economics.

Offers from:
Bristol, Durham, Nottingham, York

Engineering

The way in which things work and the reasons they behave as they do fascinate me. Recently I did a project on the London Millennium Bridge, studying the problems associated with it and the way in which they were resolved. Reading about the research the engineers conducted sparked my interest and the advances they made impressed me. "The Seven Wonders of the Industrial World", a book which narrates the stories behind some of the great engineering feats, such as the Hoover Dam, also encouraged me to look further into this subject; it seems as if the engineers involved in the projects accomplished what was thought of as impossible at the time and their knowledge and imagination really inspired me. The way in which engineering plays a vital part in so many everyday objects that we take for granted constantly amazes me. I heard a talk in which the lecturer described the reasons for the specific design of a paper coffee cup. Although this is a very simple item, it made me appreciate the thoughts behind the final product's design. It also emphasized to me just how broad this subject is and how many options it opens up for those studying it.

 Some very good and diverse aspects of engineering are described with interest and some apparent understanding.

I have thoroughly enjoyed maths and science A-level and am glad that, in view of reading engineering, I opted to take Further Maths as I have found this challenging but rewarding. The pure and mechanics modules particularly interest me and I would like to continue in this direction. Such is the breadth of engineering, however, I feel at the moment I have not had enough experience of practice in the various branches to make an informed decision about which specific route to go down. Therefore the more general university courses appeal to me, both to give me this experience and to provide a wide base on which to specialise later on. I attended a lecture on engineering which highlighted the increasing importance of a wide range of skills and indeed at Max Fordham LLP, a Building Services engineer where I did some work experience, I witnessed this. The variety of activities and projects that I faced over the week each required a wide range of abilities. I also attended a Headstart course at Newcastle University which I loved; this is what finally confirmed my decision to read engineering at university. The mix of hands on lab work and lectures appealed, as did the diversity of the topics we encountered. During my Gap year I am planning to get an industrial placement to give me further experience of engineering and would like to investigate the possibility of doing this abroad.

 The writer's enthusiasm for the appropriate abilities is usefully catalogued, but better still is the curiosity displayed, as well as the experience that has already been gained.

I play the oboe to grade 7 standard and I am a member of a large wind band at school. I find this a great opportunity to socialise and meet new people as well as providing me with a way to relax. I also enjoy working together as a group towards a goal, such as a concert, and I love the sense of achievement that accompanies this. In addition to this, I have completed my Bronze Duke of Edinburgh and am currently finishing my Gold award. Consequently my teamwork and communication skills have improved significantly, both through planning and undertaking the expeditions, and as a result of my community service, for which I visit an old peoples' home every week. This scheme has also tested my determination to complete a challenge and I have found this aspect of it very rewarding. Finally, I am Head of House and a House Prefect having joined the school only one year ago. I have therefore had to integrate quickly into an existing community; these responsibilities have increased my self confidence considerably and I hope that they will help me to develop my organisational and leadership qualities further.

 Some good demonstration of key skills such as the applicant's drive and organisation that will be useful after school.

Offer from:
Cambridge

Engineering

Engineering has always appealed to me because of my logical mind and my love of practical tasks. Ever since my first visit to Ironbridge, the site of the first cast iron bridge built by Abraham Darby in 1779, and learning about George Stephenson's "Rocket" I have been fascinated by invention and manufacture and all of the processes and toil that precede them. Of all of the different engineering disciplines I am most interested in mechanical engineering. I especially like this field because of the way in which you must apply the rules and principles of physics and maths to all sorts of everyday or specialised machines. Although I am most interested in mechanical engineering, the best thing about engineering to me is the range of different areas that you can specialise in. The engineering science course especially appeals to me as it enables all of the different areas of engineering to be explored before finally opting for one field.

This good opening paragraph demonstrates the applicant's enthusiasm for the subject. It is a very personal account that illustrates the origins and depth of interest.

The writer shows good understanding of the university course by referring to the range and variety of forms of engineering to which they will be introduced. They also indicate that they are happy to study a wide range of areas within the subject before specialising. Such indications of understanding and flexibility are likely to be interpreted by admissions tutors as evidence that the applicant is well prepared and well suited to the course.

For work experience I wanted to try an engineering job that I knew little about so I applied for a placement at an electrical engineering firm called Ultra Electronics. This experience was very valuable because not only did it cement my enthusiasm for engineering in general, but also it gave me the opportunity to work in an environment that I was not accustomed to.

The project I was working on was a light that could be used in military tanks for map reading. This was ideal as I was able to see nearly all of the different design stages as well as testing the suitability of different LED's and working with the prototypes. During the placement I enjoyed being able to offer my ideas about how to solve problems; for instance how the perspex cover in front of the LED's should be fitted so that it could be done easily by members of the production line and ensure that the join was sealed.

The applicant successfully draws the reader's attention to the fact that they have relevant work experience, and ably reinforces the

sense of enthusiasm. They go on to provide good detail through the use of an excellent example. The reader is left with a clear view that the applicant is serious and enthusiastic about the subject, and that their great interest is well founded on direct experience of actual engineering issues.

At school I attended extra classes in physics and maths; these were designed to challenge the top students and I found them very interesting as they stretched beyond the A2 syllabus. One of my favourite topics was Critical Thinking this involved a comprehension style exercise in which you analysed different passages and had to decide which statement about the passage was true; I found this very enjoyable as it was very satisfying and stimulating. I took part in the Physics Olympiad. I have also taken part in the UK Mathematics challenge, gaining a certificate every year. To me, teamwork is very important and having played rugby for the school 2nd XV for two years I have experienced it first hand. In school sport I also played for open cricket and hockey teams. As well as teamwork, my time at school has taught me other important life skills. Leadership is one of these skills, and as Head of House I had a great deal of responsibility resting on me. I found that the extra responsibility brought out the best in my personality and I thoroughly enjoyed tackling the everyday problems that are a part of school life. The Head of House has a unique position in the school as they must work very closely with the members of staff to make sure that events and general school life run as effectively as possible In order that everyone's life is made easier and happier. This communication with the staff allowed me to do my job to the best of my ability.

Maths and Physics activities beyond the syllabus are impressively catalogued, along with other useful key skills.

After I finish working I will be cycling around India with four friends raising money for an AIDS charity. I have always wanted to visit India and I wanted to do something beneficial for people less fortunate than myself.

In the last paragraph the applicant adds some good further general points that further help the reader understand the applicant's character.

Offer from:
Oxford

"Writers don't give prescriptions, they give headaches". Chinua Achebe's comment is one that I feel is relevant to almost any book that I have read. Take for example his 'Things Fall Apart'. I was left asking myself numerous questions by the end of the novel in which a range of issues concerning colonisation, many similar to those raised in Conrad's 'Heart of Darkness', are addressed. Presented with contradictory images of Africa resulting from the differing colonial European and post colonial African perspectives, I had ultimately to decide for myself how I felt about what had taken place in 'the Dark Continent'. Shakespeare's 'Othello' is another example of a work that has given me a stimulating 'headache'. The uncertainty over whether Othello's fate could have been avoided made the tragedy all the more painful for me.

Excellently business-like start, and having been plunged into the heart of the subject, the reader is then shown where Achebe's claims are true in specific texts.

Although I have observed through my reading that the questions raised by the works of writers can often be very diverse, and that styles of writing vary enormously, between as well as within periods, I have found that they all share one central aim: to make us, the readers, think. Writers do not write to provide us with answers, they write to enable us to find the answers for ourselves. The effort needed to analyse and draw accurate conclusions about literary works is what I find makes reading and studying literature so rewarding. There will always be aspects of an argument that weaken or strengthen it, but to fail to consider the various arguments and therefore reject the search would leave me feeling ultimately unfulfilled. I realise however, that in order to allow myself to make informed decisions about works of literature, I must consider the historical and theoretical frameworks within which they were created. I could have easily regarded Conrad as the 'bloody racist' that Achebe described him as, if I had failed to consider the time at which he was writing.

Although this is to the point, some of the theory repeats what has already been said in the first paragraph.

In addition to context, I feel that discussion is a vital ingredient in enabling me to make valid conclusions about works of literature. A conversation with the Scottish poet Don Patterson proved to be most useful in aiding my understanding of his work, as through it I learned how his religious beliefs had affected his ideas and poems. I have taken part in many debates about English, and these encouraged me to challenge other people's views on literature as well as defend my own. I have recently come to appreciate works of satirical writers, such as Pope and Swift, valuing the experience and knowledge that I have gained through analysing works of a genre of literature that was previously unknown to me.

Nice reference to the poet and his beliefs. Promising references to Irish literature are not supported, however, and a couple of names are just dropped in.

At school, I have been assigned the role of House Prefect, which has allowed me to develop my powers of responsibility and leadership. I am currently working towards Grade 8 certificates for Piano and Voice, which I hope to gain within the year. As a heavily involved member of the school Chamber Choir, I was given the opportunity to take part in a service held for the Queen, in addition to various live concerts and radio performances. I have also helped to produce several CDs of the choir repertoire. Although sometimes challenging and demanding, I find music a thoroughly rewarding interest, and my dedication to it resulted in my being awarded the school Music Prize.

It is only through personal consideration, discussion and appreciation of other people's views that literature can become stimulating, challenging and ultimately rewarding. As E. M. Forster once said, "Spoon feeding in the long run teaches us nothing but the shape of the spoon". I feel that the University of Edinburgh is an institution that provides the course and atmosphere that will allow me to grow and develop not only in knowledge, but also in my approach as a student of Literature, and it is for this reason that I have chosen it as my sole application.

Ideally the music and literature paragraphs would be linked.

Nice quotation to support the idea of individuality.

Very precise targeting of this piece to Edinburgh; unless you are sure of an offer, you risk any other institutions you apply to feeling second best.

Offer from:
Edinburgh

"All the lovely tales that we have heard or read: / An endless fountain of immortal drink, / Pouring unto us from the heaven's brink". Upon reading this from an extract of Keats's 'Endymion' I realised the reason for my fascination with literature. Through reading we are provided with a key into a world of immortality, a world in which anything is possible, that can be as simple or abstract as we desire. In this way literature is unique given that, having read a novel or poem, each individual will have experienced exclusively images and ideas in a way that could never be visualised exactly by anyone else. Literature is an invaluable source of information and knowledge and can teach us about the world around us. For this reason the prospect of studying English to a further level excites me, because I feel there is just so much for me to discover and explore. I am currently gripped by 'Things Fall Apart' by Chinua Achebe, which gives an insight into the culture and traditions of the Ibo tribe and challenges Eurocentric colonial images of Africa. I believe that to understand a novel it is necessary to learn about its context and background. This interests me greatly, and, having recently studied 'Hard Times' by Charles Dickens, I have realised that novels are not solely for personal enjoyment but can also play a didactic role in educating society. Achebe demonstrates this through the harm caused by the colonisation of Africa, while Dickens did this effectively by the introduction of Sissy Jupe into the Gradgrind family, to show them that love and imagination are morally and socially essential and that society was being corrupted by their materialistic, utilitarian values brought about by the Industrial Revolution.

> *Excellently appropriate and interesting opening which the writer builds on by choosing texts and detailing moments where Keats's claims for literature are demonstrated.*

To enhance my understanding of other canons of literature I am going on a school trip to Dublin where I hope to discover more about the lives and works of Irish writers. I am eager to experience the culture first hand and feel it will vastly improve my understanding of, and give me a basis for, studying Irish literature in the future.

Although I feel literature to be, ultimately, a personal experience, I believe it to be necessary for different views to be voiced and discussed in order to challenge the reader to analyse and think carefully about their reading, and by hearing the views of others your own views may be expanded. I also really enjoy theatre productions and find it intriguing to see how a director chooses to portray a play.

Having studied 'Hamlet' I went to see a modern version performed at the Old Vic, directed by Trevor Nunn, and found that the youth of both Hamlet and Ophelia had been emphasised which was something I had overlooked beforehand and I saw the relationship between them in an entirely different light.

Vague about Irish writers, although this pilgrimage does suggest commitment and enthusiasm.

Excellent precise mention of a feature of the 'Hamlet' production.

Having completed my Bronze Duke of Edinburgh award I am presently undertaking my Gold. For my final expedition I went trekking in the Atlas Mountains, Morocco, which was both an eye-opening and physically rewarding experience. I have also completed my Trident Gold award for which I gained some work experience at a law firm; I now think I would like to become a lawyer in the future and believe the skills gained from an English degree will be invaluable. To give myself a challenge I joined the school CCF for two years and attained the rank of Lance Corporal, which was a great personal achievement. I am a House Prefect and enjoy the responsibility it brings. I play a number of sports including tennis and swimming and have represented the school in lacrosse and hockey. I have attained the level of grade 4 in the clarinet and have recently taken up the piano. I have a real passion to travel and during my gap year, having worked for 5 months to earn the money, aim to go to Africa and India to embark on a conservation project. Due to being a school year ahead I feel this year out would be important for me to grow in maturity, become more rounded as a person and prepare me for a degree in literature.

The ending lacks clarity ('a school year ahead'), and the literature and travel connection are not made very directly.

Offer from:
Birmingham

"The screen is a magic medium. It has such power that it can retain interest as it conveys emotions and moods that no other art form can hope to tackle".-Stanley Kubrick. For me, this quote illustrates with clarity the unbelievable influence that film has over our lives. I believe film is a way in which one can display the feelings and emotions in a society. It is a rational form of art that expresses the feelings of certain individuals and transmits them to the audience: the power of visual representation on the human being is quite magnificent. In Plato's 'Republic', we read that he felt art and all representation was in fact so influential on the human mind that he considered it a threat to society and decided to censor it. However, Aristotle, who was taught by Plato, argued that all mimetic art offered a catharsis, and purged the soul of damaging emotions. For me cinema is a story book in motion. You can analyse the film as much as you feel is necessary and appreciate the cinematic qualities as art or as a fraud. When I watch a film, I try and understand the intellectual content and theories behind the making of it.

 Interesting on Kubrick, Plato and Aristotle; an example of a film or two that supported or contradicted the claims that are made would have iced the cake.

The reason that I want to read film studies is that for me this is a challenging discipline which raises many questions through visual representation. I have always watched film with vast admiration for the directors, script writers and the intricate planning that is so important for making a work of intellectual and social content.

I have currently been scripting a 15 minute project which I will hopefully have filmed by Easter. This project takes a look at the importance of a role model during the years of adolescence, and the film itself shows a rather dark side of the young mind in a way that explores the complexion in relationships at this age; what for one boy is a close friendship for another is an obsession. The study of French has allowed me to learn about 'la nouvelle vague', which in my opinion produced some of the best films and 'auteurs' ever. Truffaut, my favourite director, is a man who has influenced the film industry in many ways, such as in his critique of other directors, and through the various themes and theories which he introduced to world cinema. He also filmed women in a manner that was very controversial for the 1950 decade. And it is because of his works and abilities, for instance, to make an anti-hero into a character that evokes sympathy, that I have become so interested in film. His power as a director is illustrated in his debut, '400 coups' where we see a young delinquent who causes trouble wherever he is. But in a scene where he is arrested and put in a cell and the camera angle shows him in an isolated situation, and Truffaut manages to provoke a sympathetic feeling towards the young boy through the silent filming and the hopelessness of the situation that he is in. Truffaut has also inspired many acclaimed modern directors such as Tarantino. In 'Tirez sur la pianiste' there is an irrelevant and surreal conversation in a car that has nothing to do with the plot, and this is used by Tarantino in 'Pulp Fiction' where the two gangsters are in the car talking about a subject which also has nothing to do with the situation.

The demonstration of commitment and involvement with the filming process is impressive, as is the exploration of Truffaut's effects and influence.

At school, I take part in a variety of societies. These are very enjoyable because they allow me to discuss my opinions and broaden my knowledge. As well as academic study, I have played rugby and hockey at 2nd team levels and play for the football 1st team. I am a member of the School Film Society and when I can, I try to expand my film knowledge and understanding by watching as many different features as possible.

In my boarding house, I have the job of being a house prefect, and this has allowed me to take on various responsibilities. I am also head of charity within the house, which requires me to organise fun events to raise money.

More could have been made of this by giving examples of discussions to which the writer contributed and knowledge gained, and linking school activities clearly to key skills.

Offers from:
Leeds, Manchester, University College London

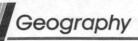

An interest in tectonics initially focused my enthusiasm for Geography, which has over the years developed into a sound fascination for the subject, especially the human components.

Excellently precise mention of plate tectonics, but the questions 'why?' or 'how?' are begged and not answered, so that the enthusiasm remains a vague claim.

Tackling controversial issues, within the A2 course, such as the changing role of the British countryside in the economy and the EU and its effect on rural communities proved to be challenging yet very exciting topics. Through the study of Tourism I have appreciated the chance to explore, in depth, the impact and particularly the complications surrounding international tourism in developing countries. In these areas I was able to combine my interest in politics, debate, ethics, travel and elements from other subjects producing a much more personal and interesting response. My broader academic interests I believe have therefore directly assisted my development as a Geographer. Over the past two years I have become fascinated in the built and architectural environment and I would love to explore this further, both from an Art Historical viewpoint and as reflection of cultural and historic advancements on society.

Within Physical Geography I continue to enjoy study and exploration of the changing appearance and nature of the landscape, developing further my A2 study of Coasts where the Dorset coastline provided a major case study. Due to the nature of the Dorset coast's lithology, structure and the impact of the 10,000Km fetch distance, sub-aerial processes and human intervention a diverse range of coastal landforms can be seen today. (These range from a double spit in Poole harbour to the Lulworth Cove and Old Harry Rocks). I found 'Coastal Systems' by Simon K. Hasslett of particular use and enjoyed exploring these areas in some depth, especially the effect and process of isostatic and eustastic movement. I am very keen to develop this interest at university through archaeology, geomorphology and glacial geology, the latter I discovered through a stimulating lecture by Geoff Green on Antarctica.

Better precision here, and the detailed description of the interesting topics in Hasslett's book shows enthusiasm beyond the narrow syllabus (which everyone has to cover anyway).

During my Gap Year I look forward to the opportunity of applying my geographical knowledge in a practical way by supporting the non-profit organisation Frontier which aims to contribute to the sustainable management of natural resources and the protection of marine wildlife in Madagascar. My role, as part of the team, will include mapping the coral beds, surveying fish and invertebrate species, work with local fisheries and educating the indigenous population on the importance of protecting their environment. During this work I aim to improve my fieldwork skills and complete a BTEC in Tropical Habitat Conservation. After this I will travel more widely looking to gain experience of the diverse range of cultures and lifestyles in Central and SE Asia. Of course all of these activities require funds and I am now in employment gaining valuable work experience and am firmly on track to earn enough money to support my plans.

I am a keen and active sports player and my major game is Lacrosse. I loved playing as part of a successful and fun first team at school and can't wait to pick the game up again at University. I have completed the Gold Trident Award and both Bronze and Gold Duke of Edinburgh Award schemes. I achieved this through a range of extra curricular activities culminating in a 10-day expedition trek through stunning scenery in the High Atlas Mountains of Morocco. It was an incredible experience that left me with a real sense of achievement. The expedition was also a valuable insight into the simplicity of rural life contrasted with the increasing dependence on tourism of cities like Marrakech. I look forward to expanding my knowledge and enthusiasm for Geography at degree level.

> *These descriptions of activities appropriate to Geography demonstrate enthusiasm and an awareness of the subject's scope and relation to the real world. They make the last third of the personal statement strong.*

Accepted by:
Durham, Exeter, Newcastle

I have lived a peripatetic lifestyle all my life, moving countries with British Council postings every 4 years or so, living most recently in Kazakhstan and Moscow. In these postings I developed a fascination with, and love of, the Russian language and culture. I think it is this exposure to other cultures, nations and people that also first prompted my interest in history. I developed a curiosity as to how events and people in the past have shaped the world today. I have had the opportunity to see the consequences of recent history, both in Swaziland just after the fall of the South African apartheid government, and in Kazkhstan during the decade after the collapse of the Soviet Union. I am fascinated by the variety of ways in which people record, interpret and analyse events, and how these differences reflect on the historian as well as on the events themselves. For example, Kazakhstanis I know, who lived through the period of change during the breakdown of the Soviet Union, expressed strikingly contrasting views on Gorbachev's role to those put forward by the western academic historians such as Alan Bullock. These conversations also impressed on me the value of the knowledge of the language in which the history is recorded (in this case Russian); much of the subtlety of expression and experience, as well as the sheer beauty of the language, can be lost in a translation.

First hand experience is an opportunity for this applicant to make the opening original, and the writer demonstrates that an interesting perspective on History has been gained.

Coming from a big family has taught me to see several points of view, and to understand that often a compromise has to be drawn. While I love argument and discussion I also relish the sheer narrative thread of the past. In medieval history, where sources are often fragmentary, the narrative is frequently less than seamless, and leaps of faith or imagination are necessary to connect events. For me there is little to match a well-told, well supported chronicle of the past, such as W. L Warren's "King John" and Peter Hopkins' "The Great Game". I enjoy reading and meeting in small groups to discuss the style, context and impact of historical works - of varying merit! Most recently I have been intrigued by Niall Ferguson's "Virtual History", in which he argues the academic value of carefully written counterfactual history.

I like the challenge of historical debate, and the opportunity to listen to specialists, such as Professor Burke and Dr Maddicott, in their fields. The interpretive aspect of history I find testing, but never dull and I also enjoy the oppertunity to debate and acess papers contributed by members.

Being a school prefect can demand shrewd negotiation between the authorities and my contemporaries, and the responsibility inherent in my duties has also nurtured my ability to make decisions and compromise. As captain of the Athletics team, I've learned that careful diplomacy has to be exercised frequently, in order to retain elite athletes who are either reluctant or needed elsewhere. However, compromise aside, I am not averse to holding strong opinions, and my facility to impose my decisions on others has been cultivated through my involvement with the school CCF. I believe that I have the determination, commitment and perseverance required for demanding study, having taken 5 subjects in my AS year, as well as enduring two seasons under the rigorous training regime of the first hockey team. As house captain of sport, I find that enthusiasm can be as vital as persistence, especially when trying to convince reluctant individuals to run in the mid winter inter-house steeple-chase competitions. I have also greatly enjoyed playing in the school's Wind bands, which have taught me the value of close teamwork, as well as an appreciation for a variety of musical styles. I really love being part of a community, which I feel has contributed a valued sense of grounding, which might not otherwise have been possible, despite the obvious advantages of a diplomatic lifestyle.

Offers from:
Durham, Edinburgh, Manchester, Nottingham, Oxford

The most chilling moment in Beethoven's Missa Solemnis involves the combination of military fanfares and drum rolls, with the words 'Miserere nobis'. The juxtaposition of this, representing disillusionment with one of the world's most powerful dictators, can only be understood in the context of history. I have been passionate about history ever since I first read a book set in the past. My voracious reading of history includes many areas outside the A-level syllabus. The American Civil War is a particular enthusiasm. The different motives behind this war are exceptionally intriguing. They are well illustrated in the compilation ' Voices of the Civil War', but especially enlightening is James McPherson's 'Battle Cry of Freedom' as it combines a worm's eye perspective with a cohesive overview. More recently, reading Jay Winik's 'May 1865', gave me an insight into the fragility of the fledgling American nation and the difficulties of post-war reconstruction.

The opening is arrestingly original, and the rest of the paragraph illustrates excellently the writer's curiosity and commitment to the subject.

My study of history pervades most areas of my life. I took up Mandarin as a result of a developing interest in the history of China. After GCSE I took a further course in German, viewing the aftermath of World War Two from a German perspective, I particularly relish discussing historical issues and analyses in the History society. I am also a keen reader of 'History Today' and I try to go to many of the exhibitions recommended. It was probably my pursuit of history outside the classroom which helped me to win the school History Prize two years running.

Other academic subjects are related well to historical affairs.

I counter-balance my academic studies with a wide range of extra-curricular activities that I plan to continue at University. At school, I played the viola for the two main school orchestras and sang in the chapel choir. I thoroughly enjoyed participating in the other artistic societies here at school, which, I hope, augmented my analytical skills as well as my genuine delight in vibrant intellectual pursuits. I was responsible for encouraging and supervising junior school debates: an enthusiasm shared is one doubled! I also had great fun playing for the school First Lacrosse team and although all of this required considerable organisation, I am always eager to take advantage of any opportunities.

 Initiative and enthusiasm are related convincingly to History.

I have begun my Gap Year by working at The Nelson Museum in Monmouth. Although this focuses on important local figures, I have appreciated the opportunity to examine documents relating to the townspeople and their lives. I plan to take a History of Art course in Venice as it represents a wonderful opportunity to fuse my passions for art, history and music - as well as learning a new language. I am also taking a Tefl course to enable me to teach in Burma next year. I have heard the world without history likened to a child without parents. Devoid of any knowledge from whence it came, it has no understanding of where it is going or how to get there. Clearly to endow history with concrete patterns so as to enable us to predict the future is questionable, yet the study of History does enable us to reflect on our society. Just as Pieter Geyl's book on Napoleon provided a thinly veiled critique of the Nazi regime so recent publications such as Norman Davies's 'Rising '44', or more obviously Niall Ferguson's somewhat anecdotal 'Empire', have interesting comments to make on today's world. I too, would revel in the opportunity to learn from history but even more, to be able to indulge in at least three years' study of my hobby and my passion.

 Again the writer's inquiring mind appropriately sees historical opportunities and lessons in the real world. An impressive ending.

 Accepted by:
Bristol, Cambridge, Durham, University College London, York

I have always been interested in how society operates and how people interact, both between themselves and in their dealings with the State, and in how rules come into being and evolve. I am particularly keen to understand how society tries to reconcile the opposition between on the one hand ensuring a minimum of social order and cohesion, and on the other protecting the freedom of the individual at both political and economic levels. This understanding becomes still more complex when different legal systems are compared. Law reflects both culture and history, strikingly illustrated in the case of English common law and French civil law. EC law demonstrates the difficulties encountered when one attempts to blend together different legal and political cultures.

> *Some intriguing ideas are floated here, but more support would have made them really impressive; in which respects do English and French law differ, for example?*

My choice of A and AS levels reflects my interests and I hope will best prepare me for my future career, i.e. one which will bring together law and languages. Ideally I would also have liked to study English language to A-level, since I like writing and found the course fascinating, but my school only offers it to AS level. I wish to study law at University, especially English and French law, and possibly Japanese law, a choice which will also enable me to use my languages to the full. I do not yet know whether to become an Academic, or else a practising lawyer, or even a journalist specialising in legal issues. Whatever my ultimate career, it will be law-based and internationally orientated. My applications are therefore fully in tune with my background and aspirations. I have been brought up in a bilingual atmosphere with comparative law and politics very often the subject of family discussions. My mother, who teaches English law, is also a translator. It is not surprising therefore that I have grown up with a love of language and writing, and an interest in law, especially from a comparative French-English standpoint. All my schooling was in France (at the Ecole Active Bilingue in Paris) from September 1990 until September 2001, when I chose to come to England to complete my secondary education. I thought that having dual British-French nationality meant more than just having two passports and speaking two languages. It also meant being at home in two cultures. Although I still get ribbed by my classmates for being part-French, especially during France-England football and rugby matches (in particular when France loses), I am very happy with the choice I made in 2001. I enjoy the teaching, the friendly atmosphere, the sporting opportunities and the feeling of being a member of a real community. I have become involved in numerous activities, (being a member of various House sports teams and the school swimming and football teams), including CCF, where I am now Cadet Corporal, and was a member of the CCF team which won the Bronze medal in the Jubilee trophy in May 2003. I am also a House Prefect, which means that I check what goes on in my school house for one day, checking people in, putting them to bed and making sure everything is in order.

Having learnt Japanese from the age of 8, and curious to learn how Japanese society really operates, I spent several weeks in the summers of 2002 and 2003 with a Japanese family in Hiroshima, and even gave English lessons to Japanese businessmen in 2003. I passed my Japanese A level in June 2004 and am preparing to sit the Japan Foundation exam at Level 2 next year. I have started studying Arabic. The language has always fascinated me and hopefully will give me some insight into the clash between Western cultures and Islam.

The linguistic credentials are strong here, although more mentions of literature would have been a good idea. This information about the candidate's desire to study law is interesting, but more demonstration of legal knowledge and curiosity would have been useful.

Offers from:
King's College London, School of Oriental and African Studies

Mathematics

Ever since I was young I have taken a keen interest in maths, and have always taken a pride in the maths I could do. In restaurants as a child I would always insist on being the one who would figure out the tip, and now I still enjoy any mathematical challenge that comes my way.

This personal anecdote begins the statement freshly and amusingly. Excellent!

Having taken GCSE maths a year early I had an additional year in which we got to work on higher, A-Level maths. After reading books such as 'Fermat's Last Theorem' by Simon Singh, 'The Magical Maze: seeing the world through mathematical eyes' by Ian Stewart, and other such books that speak about theorems which I had little prior knowledge about, such as game theory and chaos theory, I was enthralled by the world of maths. These tasters confirmed to me that maths was 'my' subject, so when it came to A-level choices I chose as much maths as was possible. In that extra year my class concentrated a lot on the purer side of maths, and as a result I have found this aspect of maths quite easy to understand and grasp. Starting mechanics was initially quite taxing, but after spending some extra time going through examples, the methods soon became clear in my mind and mechanics is now one of my favourite areas of maths.

I also enjoy physics, as I find maths and physics work together well, and I love the feeling that I have after working hard on a question (both physics and maths) when the answer emerges. Physics and maths work well hand in hand and it is satisfying when the theories learnt are put to practical uses, as they are in the engineering field. Having grown up in the Cayman Islands I have been surrounded by commerce and finance, and as a result I find myself particularly interested in the financial sector. Whether this is a result of my interest in numbers and figures, or whether this was what started my interest is a mystery. It is clear that as a result of this I am strongly considering having some form of economics in my university life.

Nice illustrations of reading beyond the compulsory syllabus demonstrate interest and enthusiasm. Background and aspirations are appropriate to the course.

Before leaving home I was very involved in community service, and was the accountant for my school's Key Club. Joining another school for 6th form has given me a chance to explore new horizons. I found the change a bit daunting at first as I was moving from a small day school to a large boarding school. I am quite an independent person and quickly settled into school. I believe that the move was not only good for me in an academic sense but also it allowed my transition into university to be an easy step. Having responsibilities of being House Charity Representative and a House Captain, I have learned to organise younger students, house activities and to manage my time effectively despite the heavy workload of A-Levels, while maintaining a healthy social life. In my free time I read, socialise, and play sport. The literature I read vary drastically between books such as Harry Potter, easy reads, to equally pleasing books like Dante's Divine Comedy (translation). As far as sports is concerned I love the game of squash, and I receive training at school and at home where played for the Island's junior squash team. It is the challenge of squash, when playing a difficult opponent, that I particularly enjoy.

I have been looking forward to university for a very long time and have put careful thought into all of the courses I have chosen and have chosen only those which I believe would be ideal for me. I would love to pursue a career within these subject areas, and I believe that my choices of institutions are on par with my capabilities as well as my future aims. Over and above the course, though, I am looking forward to the social, academic and personal opportunities that will be available at your university.

> *Some useful key skills are outlined here, but some of the material, for example the final paragraph, adds nothing to the application really and could well have been omitted.*

Offers from:
Bath, Bristol, Durham, Nottingham, Reading, Warwick

Mathematics

Three years ago I read 'The Man Who Loved Only Numbers' by Paul Hoffman and was captivated by the genius of Paul Erdos and this new perspective of Maths. I immediately sought to read other similar material and launched into Simon Singh's books. My extensive reading since then has included Keith Delvin's 'Mathematics: the New Golden Age' which has shown me the huge scope of Maths. I like all different aspects of Maths; through my reading I have seen that they all offer challenges that I delight in trying to comprehend and master. I am intrigued by the nature of numbers, the unpredictability of the primes, and the beauty of proof. Maths offers such breadth and diversity which makes it so appealing to me. All my life I have sought intellectual excellence and clarity of thought, but I enjoy Mathematics above all else.

More recently I have read 'Euler, The Master of Us All' by William Dunham, which contained Maths that was not familiar. I persevered and was able to unravel the work of a true genius. Euler clearly had on impact on all branches of Maths; but what I found particularly exciting was his proof connecting e, i and pi from the MacLaurin expansions, a truly beautiful result. I also like Maths problems, and have attempted various questions in 'Number and Proofs' by R. Allenby, as well attending a Maths club at school where we discuss aspects of the subject not found on the syllabus. This has helped me develop a particular interest in Pure Maths. I have won the school Mathematics prize for two consecutive years, as well as receiving a Gold Award in the UK Maths Challenge.

> *Extensive maths-related reading beyond the syllabus is impressive in these paragraphs, and detailed examples of the books' contents are supplied. Obviously this knowledge cannot be superficial, or the applicant will be rumbled at interview!*

I apply Maths in all areas of life. For my physics coursework, I analysed the motion of a spring completely theoretically using algebra before carrying out the investigation; more recently I have undertaken a research project into Cherenkov radiation. In politics I looked at using Probability to determine the significance of voting during the election campaign. Everywhere I look there is Maths to explore. Throughout my life I will strive to learn more about Maths, making use of it in my work, research and free time. I am very excited with the prospect of being able to study this fascinating and boundless subject at university.

Mathematics is related to the other school subjects nicely here, demonstrating the writer's interest.

I was educated in France until I was nine and as a result am fluent in French. I was awarded a scholarship to secondary school, where I am a Prefect. I am very keen on public speaking, and have frequently represented my school debating team, at the Oxford Union debating competition. I am head of academic enrichment, which involves promoting school societies and encouraging personal interests to develop. I am also a member of the International Society, the Astronomy Society and the Politics Review Society. I enjoy sharing opinions and views on all aspects of life.

I adore music and am 1st Clarinet of the school wind band and symphony orchestra. I find music a relaxing and fulfilling exercise and it also means that my time management and organisation is excellent. I love sport and play 1st team tennis and am a member of Salisbury Rowing Club, competing at national rowing competitions, as well as enjoying rugby and hockey.

I am about to finish my Duke of Edinburgh Gold award, which has involved me in many different areas of life, including undertaking a Royal Navy gliding scholarship and gaining my solo gliding qualification. I have done work experience in stockbroking, surveying, and law, offering a valuable insight into these different professions. I joined the Oxford University Astrophysics Department on an expedition to La Palma to observe Lyman alpha emissions from distant galaxies. It was hugely exciting being at the forefront of physics; I was inspired by the intensity of university life which I am looking forward to experiencing.

A clear impression of the writer's organisation, motivation and energy is conveyed in the last third of the personal statement.

Throughout the statement the writer excellently communicates passion (without deploying that over-used word!) through such strong verbs as 'captivated', 'intrigued' and 'adore'.

Offer from:
Cambridge

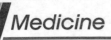
I became interested in medicine when my mother had a thyroid tumor removed. The more research I did the more my fascination in biology and ultimately the working of the human body grew.

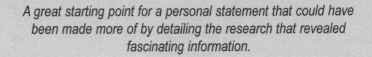

A great starting point for a personal statement that could have been made more of by detailing the research that revealed fascinating information.

I have been keen to further this interest by involving myself in a wide range of relevant work experience and service to the community. After shadowing several doctors in the obstetrics, renal, histology, radiology, and nuclear medicine departments in Kuwait Government Hospital I am convinced that the fast pace and constant advances of this discipline would suit me. In school I involved myself in community service where I worked on the Alzheimer's and Dementia ward at Savernake Hospital talking to the patients, assisting at mealtimes and during the doctors' rounds. During the last academic year I worked at the riding for the disabled centre in Marlborough. It was a pleasure to work with these children and to be able to participate in their progress. Another project was to act as a facilitator in an organic garden with people who had suffered breakdowns. The aim was to encourage them to socialize and take on increasing responsibilities within the garden and ultimately at home. Each of these activities has given me a greater understanding of the emotional plight of variously affected people. For these community placements I was awarded a school Community Service Prize.

First hand knowledge of the world of medicine is vital in medical applications, and here the writer makes the most of past experiences.

At School I was a House Prefect, Health Representative and Charity Representative. My 6th form Captaincies included Swimming, Water Polo and the Lacrosse 2nd XI team as well as representing the 1st XI squad. These commitments not only enabled me to work as part of a team, which I very much enjoyed, but also allowed me to vaunt my own dedication and responsibility in organizing events and encouraging others to participate. As a member of extra curricular societies, I presented talks to the Biology Society and to the Oxbridge Society on South Africa and Malaria respectively. I have published poetry in a school anthology and last year I won the Spanish Reading Competition.

Good evidence of key skills such as organisation and initiative is presented here.

In addition I have completed my European Computer Driving License, Trident Gold Award, and I am in the process of completing my Duke of Edinburgh Gold Award.

My year off before university will be divided into two parts. I have applied to work as a health care support worker for the NHS trust. This will not only allow me to gain more hands on experience with patients but also give me a good grounding in the workings of a hospital.

The first half will finance the second where I will be travelling to teach science in one of their rural village schools. It is my intention to introduce and run a basic health and first aid course after school hours. I also hope to visit some nearby hospitals and assist on weekends.

I have my own horse and the responsibility of his care and I compete regularly, specializing in dressage. To relax I swim and scuba dive to the level of rescue diver and emergency first responder and my next goal is to become a master diver. I have gained the St. Johns Ambulance 3 Cross Award and Life Saving to Award of Merit. I consider myself to be hard working and enjoy working with people, empathizing with them, and to be highly committed to a profession in medicine.

A list of activities and key skills that shows commitment to and some insight into the world of medicine. Important people skills are stressed.

Accepted by:
Hull and York Medical School

I see medicine as a fascinating and challenging career where learning takes place throughout your working life, as new discoveries and developments in diagnosis and treatment become available. I relish the intellectual challenge of sciences and their application in diagnosing and treating disease: for example I attended talk on HIV that dealt with the issue of how scientists go about trying to find new drugs which will stop the infection. The social implications of making treatments available such as those discussed in 'A Clone of Your Own' by Arlene Judith Klotzko intrigue me.

Interesting and well chosen specific issues start the statement off precisely.

I get great satisfaction from trying to solve problems, and if I cannot solve a problem I will keep probing at it until it begins unravelling. In physics I researched materials for the project 'Why is Titanium used in Hip replacements?' I learnt that there are many considerations to make when deciding the best procedure for a particular person and there is never just one right way of doing it. I can be resourceful and self-sufficient but I also work well in a team: for example at a Medlink course, my team won the casualty alert simulation. This gave me some insight into working as a team when you are under pressure. Medlink confirmed my medical interest and aspiration to become a doctor.

Through work experience I came to appreciate how diverse the profession is and I was able to learn more about the different environments of the hospital and GP surgery. One of the most important things that I brought away from my work experience was how patient confidentiality leads to a vital patient-doctor trust. Work experience at two hospitals gave me some insight into how hospital communities work and made me realise how important teamwork and communication with both patients and colleagues is. The real eye-openers were open heart surgery and SCBU because I was able to see how precise the work has to be. During the time I spent in the GP's surgery I was able to understand a little about patient expectations of the service and some of the dynamics of the practice. I was able to see a new computerised patient notes system when I went to the open day of a new ITU at my local hospital.

Voluntary work has been rewarding and interesting it has improved my listening and social skills with the elderly and infirm, for example when I went to help at a Christmas meal for the elderly. Once a week, I visit a lady who has cancer. I help her around the home and provide a little company for her.

> *After a credible rationale for applying to study medicine the writer gives an impressive catalogue of medical experience that shows commitment and understanding of medical issues and practice. Essential medical key skills such as team-working and the ability to relate to others are flagged up.*

I went to The Gambia on a World Challenge Expedition; for the 12 months' planning and fundraising I was the group's secretary. This helped to develop my organisational skills and made me a more succinct record keeper. I played hockey for the Oxfordshire U14-U17 teams, learning how to integrate quickly with a new group of players. County and school hockey has been fun and my contribution resulted in an Oxfordshire County award which made my time and effort worthwhile. I also have great fun playing other sports socially. I have enjoyed playing in a wind band and a school orchestra and am House Head of Music. For this I have to organise a group for a singing competition and music evenings. A career in medicine offers a wide variety of opportunities to specialise, I feel that I have the right qualities to become a good doctor and I very much look forward to starting the course.

> *Commendable organisation and commitment are displayed by the extracurricular activities, and achievements are listed in this second section.*

Offers from:
Sheffield, University College London

Modern Languages and Linguistics

The Mexican author Ignacio Padilla said: 'Every language you speak is an open door to an entire world'. It is for this reason that I have nurtured a desire to learn foreign languages. I find Spanish particularly enticing as a language. There is both the richness of the language itself and the intrigue of the passion prevalent in all Spanish culture. This manifests in the countries oldest traditions, such as the art of bullfighting, flamenco music and literature, all of which and more I have attempted to experience.I have enjoyed studying and reading Spanish literature ranging from the early short stories of Quiroga, which evoke the power of nature and the moving and sinister poetry of Vallejo (such as 'Los Heraldos Negros') to the poetic lyricism of Lorca's 'Trilogia de la Tierra' and the more recent works of Marquez which I find beautiful in their subtlety and attention to detail. Similarly I have enjoyed the uniqueness of Spanish cinema especially such films as 'El Bola' and 'Tesis' which are impressive for their dramatic impact. I have pursued my interest in all things Spanish by visiting the country many times and have taken two language courses in Nerja and Salamanca. These gave me the invaluable opportunity to live with Spanish families and improve my confidence in spoken Spanish.

> *Quoting a Spanish-speaking author is a great way to start this application, and there is much excellently precise description of the Spanish world here that shows, rather than merely claims, enthusiasm.*

I took advantage of every opportunity available to me whilst at school. This included taking Astronomy as an extra G.C.S.E subject, starting Chinese in my final year and spending the last afternoon of my school career taking the Spanish AEA exam, in which I went on to achieve a 'merit'. Furthermore I took part in many school societies which have stretched me intellectually. I recited poetry in a competition held by the 'Modern Languages Society', presented essays to a discussion group on 'Cloning' and 'Sexuality and The Church' to the 'Essay Society'. I also chaired debates throughout the school. My other main extra-curricular interest at school was music; I learnt the piano and sang both in choirs and as a solo performer.

> *Commitment and organisation are nicely illustrated here, and have bearings on the course.*

As for linguistics, it was my study towards a certificate in Mandarin which first aroused my interest. It awakened me to the great contrast between learning oriental and romance languages, I was amazed to discover for example, that Chinese verbs have no conjugated tenses. My subsequent research into linguistics includes reading 'The Language Instinct' by Steven Pinker. His questioning style made me consider the idea of whether language is a pre-programmed, instinctive art or an acquired means of communication through mimicking a parent figure.

Good support for a growing interest in this new subject.

During my final year I was made a Prefect. I enjoyed this responsibility and it reinforced my belief that I am a good listener and able to communicate with people of many different ages on a variety of levels. It has also been important to learn to juggle responsibility with academic work.

I am embarking on a trip to Mexico for five months starting this February. I will be working in a home for abandoned children situated forty kilometers north of the capital. I trust that this immersion in to an underprivileged, Spanish-speaking community will be of great value and equip me with the necessary independence and maturity to fully benefit from the onset of University life.

Valuable gap year experience in this final paragraph complements the key skills that will be useful at university.

Accepted by:
Edinburgh, Leeds, Manchester, Newcastle, St Andrews

Modern Languages - Spanish and Arabic

There is a strong utilitarian appeal to me to study Spanish, since it is a language which may possibly open up to me a large part of the world in my future professional career. It also gives access to the diversity of Spanish culture and history which I have been able to trace over the last century through reading John Hooper's "The New Spaniards". But more than anything else, I quite simply love the sound and rhythms of the language itself.

The style and beauty of a language are often most successfully captured in literature. I have read a number of Hispanic texts such as Marquez's "El Coronel" and Lorca's "La Casa de Bernada Alba". "El Coronel" in particular both animated and frustrated me. For the simplicity and fluency of his writing were a delight to read yet the ending was, I found, prosaic. My studies have allowed me to have an insight into the origins of Spanish and its development both of which greatly interest me. I have also read biographies of both Marquez and Lorca to give me an idea of the time and context in which they were writing.

I was awarded a scholarship for Spanish which I used to attend an intensive language course in Barcelona whilst staying with a native family. This allowed me (briefly) to become part of the local way of life and I was overwhelmed by the warmth and passion of the people I came to know. I have also visited the south of Spain and I discovered that despite the huge cultural difference, the nature of the people was the same.

> **❝❞** *Excellent descriptions of the literature and reasons that have inspired the application.*
>
> *The mentions of Hooper, Marquez and Lorca are nicely precise and sensitive, and the personal relationship with the host family is nicely immediate.*

I was inspired to study Arabic having witnessed the deep rooted Arabic influence in culture and architecture within the south of Spain. With Spanish already being of great interest to me, I felt encouraged to delve further into the connection between the two: I have been to see the Al Hambra in Granada (a prominent feature of the moorish presence after the Arab invasion of Spain in 711A.D.) and I have read "The Arab Conquest of Spain" by R.Collins. I was also influenced once again by considerations of my future career: I am considering the

Diplomatic Service as a profession and an understanding of Arabic would enhance the relations between any country where I might be posted and the Middle East. I am currently studying for the University of Durham certificate in Arabic as I am keen to get a year's start before going on to university. This will provide a foundation in written, oral and aural Arabic as well as a knowledge of Arab Culture.

Academic and cultural initiative and enthusiasm are demonstrated well here.

Descriptions of future plans provide a good rationale for studying languages.

I am a school prefect and won rank of Lance Corporal in CCF, and in both roles I believe I have developed my skills of leadership and my sense of responsibility. I have played 1st X1 cricket and football consistently over the past six years. I have also done a week's work experience at Nationwide where I was able to improve my IT skills by writing and sending press releases.

School achievements are concisely listed and linked to key skills.

Offers from:
Durham, Exeter, Leeds, Nottingham

Destroying the illusion that we comprehend the world perfectly, and honestly accepting the fact of our own ignorance, Socrates believed, are vital steps toward our acquisition of genuine knowledge. Philosophy puts an end to blind acceptance and allows us to distinguish a relationship between thought and reality. It exposes and challenges the assumptions which underlie our everyday thinking about the world, ourselves, our values and our beliefs. These are amongst the many reasons why I believe studying Philosophy at degree level would be time well spent.

In order to be a philosopher, I believe that one needs to treat the philosophical works one reads, not as authoritative texts to be ingested and learned, but as one side of a conversation to be participated in - there is always more beyond the page. My approach is to try to see what is motivating an argument, what unstated premises, if any, lie behind it, and how I might take the argument further. What I read is, for me, almost always the beginning of an enquiry, not the end.

I am a keen supporter of Locke's empiricist that all our ideas, simple or complex, are ultimately derived from experience. My involvement in the school Philosophy Society not only allowed me to develop my skills of argument; teaching me to express ideas in a clear, exact and literate way; but also enabled me to question my thoughts at a deeper level. I am certain that some of my ideas would have been very different, had I not had this experience. I have found the ideas expressed in the philosophical works of the great writers Plato and Descartes intellectually stimulating; in particular, Plato's treatment of love in 'The Symposium', and Descartes' views on one's own existence. I also find that arguments that I read in 'The Philosopher's Magazine', to which I am a subscriber, encourage me to think more clearly.

> *The first three paragraphs are especially strong, although mention of a good topic debated at the Philosophy Society and of a stimulating article in 'The Philosopher's Magazine' would have neatly nailed down all the claims.*

However, I realise that Philosophy cannot be confined to these texts. It is present in literature and wider culture; Samuel Beckett, for example, incorporates existentialist ideas into his play 'Waiting for Godot'. The characters Vladimir and Estragon spend the entire play waiting for salvation, in the form of Godot, to arrive, but this moment never comes. Nothing is achieved; life amounts to very little.

The effort needed to analyse and draw accurate conclusions about the ideas presented to us through philosophical works is what I find makes reading and studying Philosophy so rewarding. There will always be aspects of an argument that weaken or strengthen it, but to fail to consider the various arguments and therefore reject the search would leave me feeling unfulfilled. We can almost always learn from a close examination of an argument, even if we end up rejecting it. Even when an argument fails, there is usually at least a part of it which hits upon a truth.

An example of an argument and with details of weak and strong elements would have made this paragraph more hard-hitting.

I hope that my A level subjects of English, History and Biology will provide the right academic background for dealing with Philosophy; so that the interpretation of English, the analysis of History and the scientific aspect of Biology will come together.

Again, this paragraph is too general and hypothetical to cut much ice.

In my gap year, I will be spending several months in Argentina, working as a volunteer in a number of orphanages and care homes, as well as teaching English as a foreign language. I feel that this placement will be a wonderful opportunity for me to make a contribution, however small, towards improving the lives of other people. By the time I leave Argentina, I hope to have made a significant difference.

Offers from:
Edinburgh, Leeds, Newcastle, Nottingham, Oxford Brookes

Philosophy Politics and Economics (PPE)

What really stimulates me is how subjects relate to each other, how they interact and where the indeterminate areas between them are, which is what I find interesting about PPE. I have been reading both 'Think' by Simon Blackburn and 'Problems of Philosophy' by Bertrand Russell and these books, and some of my other reading have all sparked off my interest in the field of Epistemology. What particularly struck me was the difference of opinion particularly over how reliable experience is as a basis for knowledge, as opposed to the ideas of knowledge through the principles of mathematics and logic. I was inspired by Bertrand Russell's justification of Philosophy in 'Problems of Philosophy', which has led me to desire to learn about the world around me. How much I once took as certain, without any justification, now astounds me. We can take apart our own basic assumptions and look beyond. Colour vision, for example, is a thought provoking topic, which has forced me to regard the world in an entirely different light.

My interest in politics was sparked mainly by my idealistic nature. Deploring the decisions of government, I now wish to understand the system in order to explain and find new and better forms of government. Aristotle's view on different governments I find particularly thought provoking, along with Rousseau's contractual theory of government. Economics in contrast has come to me through a combination of curiosity as to what the news stories meant when discussing, for instance, the Internet bubble and a desire to understand the forces that help shape our world. It has also served as an outlet for my desire to create models and hypotheses to explain how things operate. In John Kay's book 'The Truth about Markets' I was very interested to see the overlap between the statistical and mathematical side of logic, and the use of these ideas in a practical application in Economics. Reading about the interaction of geopolitical factors in shaping the worlds economy, as well as the ideas of spontaneous organisation, and morality and ethics in the market place really sparked my interest. How political decisions affect the economy and vice versa have given me an understanding of how we can affect, in both constructive and destructive ways, the complex system of global markets. This showed me how much philosophy has implications for us in the real world.

How our methods of logic and morality affect our political and economic dealing fascinates me and has been fed to a great extent by my History. Studying the evolution of the British parliamentary system through the civil war and the reform acts that followed has led me to a much greater understanding of politics today. Learning about the formation of democracy and how important parliamentary privilege is really opened my eyes. And my interest in Marxism, which has evolved through off-syllabus reading, combined with a study of the French revolution has given me an interesting window into different political ideologies and their implications, as well as into how economic conditions can shape our lives, and how powerful a philosophical idea or theory can be.

Reflection on the nature of this combination of subjects is supported by excellent evidence of the writer's inquiry beyond the syllabus.

I have taken up every challenge that I have come across, my greatest achievement being completing the Devizes to Westminster canoe race and at a close second climbing a 6000m high Himalayan peak in northern India. These have taught me self-reliance and self-belief. As well as these accomplishments I am finding an increasing enjoyment of teaching. I am qualified as an RYA sailing instructor, and have been teaching for two seasons now, working with all age groups and the disabled regularly. I have taught as a badminton and outdoor activities instructor. These have helped me develop leadership and communication skills as well as organisation, teamwork and learning how to handle responsibility. I am also active in the school debating team, something that I have a real love of, helping run training sessions as well as participating in national competitions.

A concise description of skills that will stand the writer in good stead on his course at university concludes the statement nicely.

Offers from:
East Anglia, Lancaster, Oxford, Warwick, York

A belief shared by many, and one to which I also subscribe, is that over the past few centuries we have only just managed to grasp the fundamentals of the universe. The realisation that there is so much more to explore in science has truly captivated my imagination. I have always had a great desire to have my understanding of a subject developed and challenged, and to have the opportunity to learn new ideas and theories concerning the world around me; studying physics at university would be hugely fulfilling.

 A relevant but rather vague opening. Who are the 'many' who share the belief, exactly? Some examples of the newly-grasped fundamentals would have made the claim more convincing.

Studying physics at AS level inspired me to explore further into and beyond the course. Subsequently, reading Bryson's 'A Short History of Nearly Everything', though it is a little superficial, has allowed me to realise that there are many fascinating areas in physics I know very little about. His chapters on atoms and quarks encouraged me to read further into this topic. 'The Discovery of Subatomic Particles' by Weinberg, although written a little over 20 years ago, provides an immensely interesting and approachable introduction to this subject. As a regular reader of New Scientist magazine, I have also found many articles of huge appeal. One such article led me to read 'The Emperor's New Mind' by Roger Penrose encompassing not just Artificial Intelligence but also a range of other extremely interesting topics such as Heisenberg's 'Uncertainty Principle'.

In addition to reading, I attended a fascinating lecture at Oxford speculating on evidence for the creation of the moon which, although advanced, proved of great inspiration for me. I am a member of a physics 'extension class', a discussion group for critical thinking and problem solving, and have given a presentation on 'Kevlar' and its remarkable properties to my peers. Aside from physics, maths (I grasped the opportunity to take fifteen units) and chemistry are also subjects I have a keen interest in; both these subjects have overlapped with each other and physics throughout the A-level course so far. This has allowed me to appreciate, for example, being able to apply exponential functions and differential equations learnt in maths, as well as models of the atom taught in chemistry, to my understanding of physics. I have also attended both maths and chemistry 'extension classes' to expand my knowledge further in those areas.

Reading and lectures are impressively described in detail here, demonstrating curiosity and a willingness to go beyond the narrow confines of the compulsory school syllabus.

Opportunities for responsibility within my school, such as Chapel Representative (a role in which I give weekly presentations on morals and ethics to the first years), House Prefect, I.T representative and Health Education representative, have all helped me expand on my leadership skills, organisation and self discipline. In March 2005 I achieved one of the most challenging and rewarding experiences of my life by completing the Devizes to Westminster Canoe race. From it, and through my commitment to CCF and team sports, I have learnt a great deal about myself and how to communicate and work well with others. I plan to take a gap year after A-Levels and hope that this will give me the chance not only to work at a company in Boston, America, which deals with the design, manufacture and testing of a wide range of products but also to travel as widely as my savings allow.

 School activities are linked to key skills that will be useful at university and beyond. The gap year has a technical and scientific aspect to it, which is nicely appropriate to the course.

 Offers from:
Bristol, Durham, Leeds, Oxford, Southampton, Warwick

My passion for politics was first aroused when I became politically aware around the age of fifteen. My interest in following current affairs and an inspirational politics teacher motivated me to develop my political understanding. In addition, I have an ambition to pursue a career allied to politics, such as policy advice. Politics is fascinating both in a historical and current context.

Begins with enthusiasm, but more detail would improve it - what exactly was it that sparked the political passion? Precisely how did the teacher inspire?

I have particularly enjoyed developing an understanding of subjects such as the nature of the British Constitution. Whilst reading 'The Hidden Wiring' by Peter Hennessy, I became aware of one of the most neglected subjects in politics: it seems strange that we have lost sight of our vague and somewhat flawed constitution. Hennessy uses examples like QPM, The Nolan Report and Bagehot's 'British Constitution' in order to convince the reader of the existence of a constitution. Personally, I am more skeptical of our 'uncodified' constitution than Hennessy is and it strikes me as quite eerie that the government can merely guillotine bills through Parliament thus avoiding any intensive scrutiny. On the other hand, if one looks at how cumbersome and inefficient the American system is, it throws doubt over the practicalities of implementing a 'codified' constitution.

Reading is a pastime which gives me particular pleasure. In relation to politics, I have tried to choose my reading constructively to further a better understanding of the course. For example, Peter Hitchen's 'Abolition of Liberty', which offers an accessible, if disturbingly right wing, account of how, over the last 50 years, the country's Legal and Penal systems have declined in importance. However, the topic which is of particular interest to me is Harold Wilson's final administration: reading the memoirs of Bernard Donoughue and Joe Haines gave me an appreciation of a rather more turbulent time in British Politics than that of today. Donoughue's autobiography was able to give me guidance in gaining further information about the work involved in policy advice, a career which couples extensive academic research with competition based upon skill and ability rather than political alliance - Donoughue claims that, until he became chief policy advisor, he had no strong connections with any party.

When the writer shifts to books on the constitution the focus is clearer, and the curiosity and understanding are tangible.

Although I enjoy reading political matter, I am also an avid reader of fiction. I am a great fan of the works of Turgenev such as 'Sketches from a Hunter's Album' and 'First Love'. The former serves as a seminal - and unfortunately underrated - social condemnation of pre-emancipation Russia and the latter as a story of masculine emotion, which proves much more poignant than Goethe's 'The Sufferings of Young Werther'. Having said this, I am also a great fan of James Baldwin and Gore Vidal. Who, in my view, are two of the finest writers of the 20th century with their important work on crushing the unnecessary sexual and moral taboos that were rife in America during the fifties and sixties.

At school I contribute to the literary and satirical magazine. I have certainly been enthused by my experiences and working within journalism is certainly an area I would like to explore in the future.

Literary and journalistic paragraphs emphasise skills that are appropriate to the course.

For me the key attraction to politics is the fact that it is such an organic subject. Ever developing, it requires you to keep abreast of current affairs and the happenings of Parliament in order to stay ahead of the game. I believe that I have the interest and desire required to make a positive input into a Politics course at university and hope to make use of my studies in my future career.

This ends nicely with course-specific claims, but the writer does not really need to declare his interest and desire - they have already been demonstrated in the middle paragraphs.

Offers from:
Leeds, Newcastle, Queen Mary London

Two events occurred which confirmed my feelings and provoked a strong interest in studying International Relations at university. The first was when I attended a lecture on 'The Surgical Consequences of the Siege of Sarajevo', only to find that I came away more captivated by the reasons that lay behind this dreadful episode than by the nature of the medical casualties which it caused. The other was when on a cricket tour I spent some time in the Alexandra Township in South Africa. This was a truly disturbing experience, as I saw at first hand the persisting consequences of apartheid and at the same time the real hunger the children had for education.

 Strong personal reasons for studying the subjects begin the statement freshly.

The Balkan Wars have been followed in more recent years by the 'Crisis of Islam', and I have followed carefully the apparently growing clash between Christian and Islamic cultures. Books I have read on this topic include 'The Middle East: 2000 Years of History from the Rise of Christianity to the Present Day' by Bernard Lewis, and this is an interest which I should like to pursue in my university studies.

The future of Africa continues to interest me greatly, and on this I have read Nelson Mandela's 'In His Own Words; From Freedom to the Future'. For three or four months in my Gap year I shall go back to the Alexandra Township to teach, and I hope at that time to find out more about the problems and conflicts of this society.

 Gap year plans show a committed interest to politics, as well as the key skills of organisation and sensitivity (along with a praiseworthy charitable streak).

The study of History has introduced me to the political and economic forces that shape human events, and I very much want now to understand (if that is possible) how these forces are working in our present political climate. I am a regular reader of the International Herald Tribune, and my general reading on international relations has recently included Jackson & Sorenson's 'Introduction to International Relations: Theories and Approaches' and 'The Globalization of World Politics' by J Baylis and S Smith. It is very striking to see how closely the affairs of any one state are bound up so tightly with those of another. I believe that to study this subject to degree level will allow me a great insight into how the international community works, as well as give me the opportunity of studying politics in both regional and global arenas. I want to examine the critical issues of modern times; the changing nature of international cooperation and conflict, the impact of globalization upon states and societies and the persistence of world problems such as poverty.

I have travelled widely, visiting countries in North and South America; staying with local families in Argentina and Uruguay, Europe and Southern Africa as well as spending a month touring around China, which really allowed me to see the contrast of East and West in one country. At school I was a member of the Historical and Political Societies, and these allowed me to develop my understanding by listening to guest speakers and discussing various topical issues. I enjoyed playing many team sports and I was a member of the 1st XV rugby team and the 1st XI hockey, cricket and soccer teams. I believe that the friendship and camaraderie that one gains from playing in a sports team can last a lifetime and I have been lucky enough to have played with boys from around the country in the South of England Hockey team and in the Hampshire county rugby team.

I was a school prefect, an honour which allowed me to gain the experience of significant responsibility within the school community.

> *Overall, impressive wide reading of much topical work in Politics and International Relations is convincingly followed up with details of what exactly was learned from it.*

Offers from:
Leeds, Leicester, Liverpool, Newcastle

Psychology

It was studying English Language at AS that first aroused my interest in the psychology of journalism and advertising; I found it intriguing how the cunning use of linguistics stimulated artificial desires. I wanted to learn how and why this works.

Work-experience at a television production and post-production company gave me the opportunity to learn about the techniques used to promote products to specific consumer groups. Attending Biology Symposiums and Biological societies held at school, I first encountered some possible psychological explanations. Pursuing my growing interest I read introductory books on psychology and was recommended Oliver Sacks' 'The Man Who Mistook His Wife For A Hat'. I became absorbed in the psychological and neuro-physiological descriptions of each mental condition.

Another inspiration for me was Mark Haddon's 'The Curious Incident Of The Dog In The Night-Time'. I was struck by the fact that this boy's mathematical ability was greatly underestimated by those around him due to his lack of social skills. This description of Asperger's Syndrome helped me also to appreciate the problems that general ignorance of a condition can cause to sufferers and their families.

The writer's initial impulse to study Psychology is a great way to open. Detailed and specific references to ideas show genuine interest and enthusiasm.

My work with the Riding for the Disabled Association has enabled me to observe at close hand the impact that mental and physical impairment have on peoples lives, and the benefits that working with animals has in improving communication, learning skills and general happiness. I enjoy working with the children and find it hugely rewarding. I hope also to gain experience with slightly older children closer to my age from a different culture and social background when doing voluntary work in a school in rural Malaysia teaching 13 to 18yr olds for five months.

I believe that studying A-level Maths I developed logic and problem solving skills. This also helped my proficiency in data interpretation and analysis in the A-level Biology course practical experiments. Aspects of my A-level Art stimulated my developing interest in Psychology. In my coursework I explored the relationships between perceptions of beauty and how the mind works. One example that intrigued me in particular was the use of the 'Golden Ratio' in certain works of art, and why it makes a picture more pleasing to the eye.

The writer nicely relates A-Levels to appropriate aspects of a Psychology course.

Being appointed a school prefect gave me valuable experience in communicating with both the pupils and teachers. I thrived on organising people and events where I had to show leadership qualities while also performing as an active part of the prefect team. These included dances for younger pupils and charity events.

At school I played both the cello and the piano to grade 8 level and took part in the school's Symphony and Chamber Orchestra, while also representing my school in open hockey and tennis teams. I enjoyed a lot of what school had to offer but had to develop the skill and stamina to juggle all my commitments.

Since leaving school I have put most of my time and effort into equestrian eventing, which is a sport I have always been passionate about. I was thrilled to qualify for the under 21 National Championships after being placed in the top three at the South-East of England Regional Championships. Since then I have been building on this success and hope to continue my equestrian career on my return from Malaysia.

Key skills such as organisation, drive and initiative are usefully and concisely catalogued.

Accepted by:
Edinburgh, Exeter, Manchester, Newcastle

My growing understanding of science and my fascination for it is changing the way I look at the world we live in. A lecture by Dr. Vukusik of Exeter University on colour and light triggered a great interest for the subject; he delivered a comprehensive yet comprehensible talk on how light interacts with the energy levels of electrons in atoms to produce colours. Inspired by this I began to look at the way light and colour are related in more detail, and in what way absorption and emission spectra of different materials are related to their electron arrangements. This led to my doing a project on light in the atmosphere, and how it scatters and interferes to produce different colours.

Personal reasons for studying Science kick the statement off convincingly, and the inspirational lecture is nicely detailed.

I have enjoyed how chemistry, mathematics and physics have overlapped at AS; areas such as electron behaviour and quantum mechanics especially interested me and the opportunity afforded by a Natural Sciences course of studying physics, chemistry and maths is particularly attractive to me. My interest in quantum mechanics led me to read "In search of Schrodinger's cat" by John Gribbin. It was enlightening to see how quantum theory was, at the time, so shockingly different to how anyone had ever looked at the world, and how fundamental the flaws in classical physics were. I was also intrigued by how it portrayed a theory never to be complete: the continuous reshaping of the model of the atom, from the ones provided at A level study such as Rutherfords and Bohrs, to more complicated ones such as Schrodinger's. While the uncertainty of these theories does make me feel uneasy, I am highly excited by the prospect of immersing myself in the study of such abstract ideas. The mathematical content of the course definitely attracts me: I enjoy the tidiness of pure mathematics and how it enables scientific problems to be solved easily. This problem solving aspect of further mathematics, with its strictly logical nature challenged my mind in ways it hadn't been before and affected the way I look at science. I've greatly enjoyed reading about science; "The Birth of the Living Universe" by Gribbin I found particularly intriguing in the way it related the chemistry of human life to astrophysics. I've also enjoyed reading articles from New Scientist and Nature magazines. Studying history I believe has improved my analytical skills. It has taught me to argue theoretically as well as rationally, and to not necessarily agree with everything, but to use my own opinion.

An excellent collection of experiences and detailed explanations of what was learned. Only the articles from New Scientist and Nature are left vague.

I was lucky enough to have gained work experience for a company called Foseco in Hengelo, Holland. This involved helping researchers find chemicals for use as coatings for iron castings: this required an understanding of polymer physics and chemistry. I thoroughly enjoyed working in the laboratory environment and this helped me decide to pursue study at undergraduate level in experimental science.

I spent one week last summer working voluntarily for a disabled children's charity called "Activenture". I found this challenging but greatly rewarding, in that it involved looking after the children 24 hours a day. Despite my heavy workload, I still find time at school to organize a hectic extra curricular life. I am a keen football player, and play for the school 1st X1, and have recently taken part in the world youth Gothia Cup in Sweden. I play many sports and take part in the CCF. I am a House Prefect and am enjoying this opportunity of developing my leadership and organisational skills.

Work Experience suits the course, and extracurricular activities that demonstrate such key skills as organisation are concisely catalogued.

Offers from:
Cambridge, Durham, St Andrew's, University College London

Sports Science

My interest in playing sport has triggered a curiosity in sports physiology and a desire to understanding the social and scientific reasons which motivate and enable sportsmen to achieve excellence. I hope that by studying sports science I will be able to develop my interests as well as have the opportunity to pursue my own sporting ambitions.

 This paragraph is vague and logically rather circular (interest in playing sport triggers desire to study the subject which will fuel the interest in playing sport). Better to have recounted a moment of particular interest that happened during a game that the writer participated in or watched, and then to have progressed to an interest in the theory behind the activity.

The combination of A level PE and Biology has allowed me to explore the importance of exercise physiology, biomechanics and nutrition in relation to sporting performance. The physiological effects of training were of particular interest, especially relating to energy systems where I was able to apply my understanding to my personal exercise programme, based on developing acceleration over 20m. I have also been able to apply the science of biomechanics to many of my sports, in particular golf and tennis.

 More on the contents of the university course would have strengthened this first section.

In order to gain the broadest possible understanding of the role that exercise and sport plays in society I have taken the opportunity to participate in as many supporting activities around my academic schedule. In my age group I have represented the school at the highest levels in all team sports (rugby, hockey and cricket), but have tried to expand my interest by studying and participating in individual sports as well (tennis and golf). As well as participating in sport I have had experience of administrating and organising it within the house system at school: this has strengthened my desire and has encouraged me to continue with it academically at university. Being Head of Sports and house prefect has helped me attain certain qualities such as communication and leadership which I hope will be of use to me when studying at undergraduate level. I have also used my spare time out of the school environment to develop my knowledge and understanding of the sporting world. Over the last two summers I have worked for an events management company at a number of top class sporting events, such as the British Golf Open and the recent Ashes test. First hand experience of these events and personal contact with elite sportsmen has further inspired me to study how success is achieved in sport. This experience has given me further insight into the psychology, management and atmosphere of elite sport, all of which I am intrigued by. I will be continuing with the events management company at the beginning of my gap year to raise money for a trip to Thailand.

I have had experience in coaching sports as well. I chose hockey coaching as a service for my Dof E award as I represent the school first team. It involved me directing and training the youngest teams in the school, boys and girls, once a week. It interested me how skill levels, strategies and team cohesion differed between age groups and genders; this altogether benefited my ability to analyse sporting situations.

After I complete my A levels I intend to embark upon a gap year. I am in the process of organising a placement in Thailand working at the Suphanburi sports school, located 3 hours north of Bangkok. The school is one of twelve provincial schools for children in Thailand with outstanding sporting talent. At Suphanburi I would be a volunteer working alongside coaches and students helping with training sessions, matches and tournaments. I have chosen this type of work as I want to help nurture talent in a different culture. I believe that I could benefit from this experience hugely.

I believe that the qualities evident in sportsmen are all qualities that can lead to a successful and fulfilling life. I believe I have many of these qualities already which attendance at university will hone and focus.

An impressive blend of first hand playing and coaching experience and knowledge of professional sport.

The second two thirds of the statement are stronger than the first, and if the order had been reversed the statement would have been even more impressive.

Offers from:
Bath, Birmingham, Brighton, Edinburgh, Exeter, Leeds

I would find studying Theology both intellectually challenging and thoroughly enjoyable. I believe that the wide range of skills taught within the subject such as historical analysis, textual and literal criticism, learning an ancient language and comparative techniques will contribute to a truly motivating course. My enthusiasm for Theology was prompted during the AS coursework, for which I wrote an essay on whether or not Christianity has changed over time, focusing on gender equality. This not only expanded my interest in the topic area but also gave me an insight into the skills needed for the subject, as well as teaching me how to sustain a line of argument throughout an essay.

Good knowledge of the course is displayed, along with understanding of the skills required.

I am studying German for A2 as it will be especially useful to be able to research the works of many of the great theologians and philosophers in their own language. I am very keen to take part in the Erasmus scheme and live in Germany for a year, studying Theology. German has taught me key language skills as well as literary skills, which I can transfer into theology. Doing Maths for A level has refined my initiative and problem solving skills, and similarly, an AS level in Geography has significantly improved my analytical, comparative and statistical skills. All of these subjects have proved very useful in my study of Theology so far, as well as being very stimulating in their own right. This year, I will also be taking a certificate in Arabic, thus improving my technique in learning non-Romance languages, which I hope to study in the course.

This paragraph, which is only indirectly connected to Theology, could have been relegated to a lower position than the next paragraph which is more clearly connected to the subject and displays excellent initiative and interest.

Last term I founded the school Theology Society, for which I am currently working on a presentation called 'The Quest for the Historical Jesus,' a topic area in which I am particularly interested, as it combines both Biblical studies and elements of the philosophy of religion. For this topic area, I have read a variety of books, such as G. Theissen's, 'In the shadow of Jesus', G. Vermes' 'The Changing Faces of Jesus' and E.P. Sanders' 'The Historical Figure of Jesus'. I am also researching texts by theologians such as Schweitzer and Wenham. Along with this, I am a member of the school scholars society, in which I both give talks and debates on contemporary issues, as well as listening to others speak on a fortnightly basis.

I am a committed member of the Combined Cadet Force and the Swindon rowing club. As a Sergeant in the CCF I am responsible for the fifteen cadets in my section, and instruct them in a range of skills, from weapon training to drill, as well as leading them on exercise. This requires a high level of initiative as well as leadership and communication skills, which I am continuously developing. Rowing in a double has taught me about teamwork and also about commitment as competing often involved getting up at 5:30am some mornings to train in the weeks before regattas.

Within my house I have a variety of positions of responsibility, which have been very enjoyable. As house chapel representative I give a talk once a week to the lower years, focussing on issues such as trust, communication and relationships. This pastoral role is complemented by my position as head of the 3rd Form, for which I provide an alternative to the house staff if and when the youngest house members need any advice or help concerning school and social life. Combined with my role as a House Prefect, these positions mean I am in constant and close contact with both members of staff and the lower years, strengthening my communicational skills.

I am hoping to spend my Gap year in Germany in order to become fluent in the language and to develop strong links with the country - I am keen to return there throughout my time at university and afterwards. A gap year will also enable me to mature both culturally and socially as a student in a foreign language school, permitting me to maintain my academic interests, whilst also allowing me to enter university refreshed or the next phase of my education.

> *Useful key skills are catalogued above, and a gap year plan which has relevance to the language component of the course. A good way to sign off.*

Offers from:
Durham, Edinburgh, Leeds, Manchester, Nottingham, St Andrew's

Veterinary Science

My natural scientific curiosity along with an affinity with animals have inspired me to want to study veterinary medicine. To further my knowledge I have gained extensive experience in the field of animal health. This has enhanced my interest, and I am attracted to the profession's search for solutions to problems and its continually evolving nature. I qualified as a Marine Mammal Medic and put these skills to use while working for a month in Canada assisting with the rescue and rehabilitation of seals and other wild animals. The treatment of undomesticated animals requires skills that differ considerably from those required when working with household pets. It is vital that wild animals remain wary of those that treat them.

In contrast I have overseen practice at a small animal clinic for two weeks and spent two weeks at Equine Hospitals. I noted that a proportion of the vet's skill was in relating to owners and advising them as to the best course of treatment for their animals in their specific situation. The work I do as a volunteer for my local Riding for the Disabled Group has developed my communication skills with both the children in the group and with other volunteers.

I spent a week lambing and two weeks on a dairy farm (milking, and returning later in the year to help with calving). This I enjoyed immensely from the perspective of a prospective veterinary student gaining much 'hands on' experience. However I was alerted for the first time to the economic choices a farmer must make in order to run a farm as a business, for instance, the decison to cull free-martins. This closely related to my visit to an abattoir that helped my understanding of the link between human and animal health.

Spending a week with exotic pets at Notcutt's Garden Centre inspired my interest in animal behaviour in artificial situations. A week at a racing yard highlighted this and enhanced my awareness of the differing techniques used to get different animals to peak fitness.

> *Excellent personal and practical experience - essential to Veterinary Science applications - is flagged up here from the middle of the first paragraph.*

To assist in my Physics coursework I became involved with research in the Physics Department of Exeter University studying the optical effects of a butterfly's wing and I have also completed in Biology an extensive project on the use of surrogacy in transgenic sheep.

I attended courses at Nottingham and Cambridge aimed at prospective vet students. Here I practised simulated keyhole surgery and the realities of being 'on call'. These experiences tested my ability to work under pressure.

At school I have set up conservation initiatives and been House Prefect and Head of Choir, positions requiring me to lead others. Completing my Gold Duke of Edinburgh's Award has enabled me to work as part of a team as has representing my school 1st team in Athletics and Lacrosse. I am currently preparing for my Pony Club 'A' Test and have evented my horse up to the highest junior level. I believe I would be well suited to a veterinary career, as I am enthusiastic and committed to animal welfare. In learning to manage my time to fit in extra-curricular activities as well as balancing academic demands I feel I am left well prepared for the challenges of university life.

An excellently appropriate series of experiences is listed, along with what the writer learned from them. It all demonstrates commitment and a clear idea of what the training will involve.

Offers from:
Bristol, Liverpool, Royal Veterinary College

Index

Index

degree course descriptions

Over 120 experts on hand to help

Students need to know what's relevant to them about the nature of the degree courses they are considering. They do not want either waffle or hype.

Degree Course Descriptions will tell them much of what they need to know.

Covering over 120 of the most popular degree course areas and written by heads of department and senior lecturers at major universities, these people know the courses from the inside. They also understand the doubts and difficulties facing students who are about to make choices that will affect their whole lives.

Everything at the fingertips on one or two A4 sheets

Thoroughly revised and updated, the **2006/7 edition** of **Degree Course Descriptions** is now available.

Each description can be viewed onscreen, or printed out to give:

- a wide-ranging overview of the course

- details of the structure of each course

- career opportunities for graduates

- related degrees

- recommended reading

- recommended websites - updated and expanded to include UK and Irish websites

- a 20-point course checklist
  Students can assess their own suitability using a series of 20 relevant questions based on interests, abilities and personal qualities

For more information

For the latest information on pricing and availability please contact COA directly by phone **01362 688784** or email **orders@coa.co.uk**

opening doors of opportunity